BASIC CONCEPTS IN MUSIC

GARY M. MARTIN
University of Oregon

SECOND EDITION

WADSWORTH PUBLISHING COMPANY
Belmont, California
A division of Wadsworth, Inc.

TO MY WIFE

for her love,

support, and

encouragement.

Music editor: Sheryl Fullerton

Editorial and production services: Cobb/Dunlop Publishers Services, Inc.

© 1980 by Wadsworth, Inc.

© 1966, 1975 by Wadsworth Publishing Company, Inc. All rights reserved. No part of this book may be reproduced, stored in a retrieval system, or transcribed, in any form or by any means, electronic, mechanical, photocopying, recording, or otherwise, without the prior written permission of the publisher, Wadsworth Publishing Company, Belmont, California 94002, a division of Wadsworth, Inc.

Printed in the United States of America

1 2 3 4 5 6 7 8 9 10–84 83 82 81 80

Library of Congress Cataloging in Publication Data

Martin, Gary M.
   Basic concepts in music.

   Includes indexes.
   1. Music—Theory, Elementary—Programmed instruction.
I. Title.
MT7.M365   1980   781'.07'7   79-20496
ISBN 0–534–00761–9

Contents

Introduction
[1]

1 Basic Components of Music Notation
[4]

Staff and Grand Staff
Treble Clef and Bass Clef Signs
Bar Lines and Measures
Time Values of Notes
Time Values of Rests
Pitch Levels of Notes
Performance Markings and
Dynamic Markings
Musical Calligraphy

2 Basic Components of Rhythm
[58]

Components of Rhythm Identified:
e.g., pulse, meter, tempo
Mathematical Relationships
of Musical Notes
Tied Notes, Dotted Notes, Slurred Notes
Meter Signatures and How They
Determine Measure Content
Simple and Compound Meters
Pickup Notes
Accent, Staccato, Tenuto,
and Slur Markings

3
Basic Components of Pitch
[123]

Definition of Pitch
Names of Notes in Treble Clef
Names of Notes in Bass Clef
Sharps, Flats, Naturals
Octaves
Names of Notes on Piano Keyboard
Half Steps and Whole Steps

4
Harmonic Structure of Music
[198]

Definitions of Harmony, Chord, Triad and Interval
Identity of Basic Intervals
Concept of Major and Minor Thirds
Harmonic Intervals and Melodic Intervals
Construction of a Triad
Major and Minor Triads
Inversions of Intervals and Chords

5
Major Scales, Chords, and Keys
[248]

Definitions of Key, Key Tone, Tonality, Scale
Position of Half Steps in Major Scales
Characteristics of Notes in Major Scales
Tonic sol-fa System
Circle of Fifths for Major Keys

Major Key Signatures
Chord Names
Characteristics of Major Chords

6
Minor Scales, Chords, and Keys
[311]

Differences Between Major and Minor Scales, Chords, and Keys

Two Different Kinds of Minor Scales

Circle of Fifths for Minor Keys

Relative Major and Minor Keys

Characteristics of Minor Chords

The i, iv, and v Chords in Minor Keys

Tonic sol-fa System in Minor Keys

7
The Structure of Music
[354]

Definitions of Motive, Phrase, Period, and Sequence

Phrases, Motives, and Periods in Musical Context

Definitions of Binary (Two-Part) and Ternary (Three-Part) Song Forms, Free Form, and Examples of Their Use in Musical Context

Common Cadences

Relationship Between Cadences and Phrases

Appendix
[394]

Song Index
[397]

Index of Terms
[398]

Preface

Many students arrive in introductory music courses with inadequate understandings of fundamental musical principles. Furthermore, their widely varied musical backgrounds have produced individual "gaps" that seldom coincide.

Basic Concepts in Music is designed to provide the specific knowledge each student lacks in order to bring the class to a uniform level of understanding from which the teacher may proceed. The book format has been carefully tested and revised to perform this function. A "branching" program tests the students' understanding of each concept before it is explained. Thus, students who can answer the *Diagnostic Question* for a particular concept move quickly to the next one. If they cannot answer the question, they receive either a short review of the subject or a lengthy explanation, according to their self-determined need. Students spend time only on the concepts they don't understand, working always at their own speed and at their own levels of understanding.

Five features the author has found lacking in most introductory music books have been incorporated into this text:

1. **A careful presentation of music fundamentals.** Study is organized in units that cover the basic components of music notation, rhythm, melody, harmony, intervals and chords, major and minor tonalities, and structure (that is, phrase, motive, period, and binary and ternary forms).

2. **An exciting approach to programmed instruction.** Concepts are presented in small steps as in linear programs, but there are several alternative routes through the material, each with a different mode of presentation. The diverse techniques used in explanations and tests are intended to avoid the "pall" effect, which is inflicted on students and teachers alike by endless statements of facts, page after page or frame after frame.

3. **Skill builders.** Knowledge unlocks doors and gives us new capabilities, but only when we apply that knowledge in some activity are our capabilities fully realized. For this reason, every chapter concludes with special activities that allow the student to bring the concepts into action.

4. **Self-tests.** Placed at the end of each chapter, these tests reinforce the students' knowledge, reveal the areas that still need review, and thereby teach as well as evaluate.

5. **Review indexes.** Combined with the self-test answers at the end of each chapter, the index refers students immediately to a part where they can review the test questions just missed.

Many undergraduate college students who use this book express enthusiastic approval with such comments as:

- These chapters served as a very good review, as I found that I had forgotten a lot. . . .
- . . . an interesting way for such a large class to become equated in musical knowledge in a fairly short time. . . .
- . . . more a game than a chore. . . .
- The chapters have been interesting, and I like moving at my own pace.

Music, of course, is an art that must be heard to be appreciated. The individual who desires to broaden his or her musical understanding must become involved with sound. Perhaps the best any book can do to further musical understanding is to bring greater meaning to the creation and perception of those musical sounds. Correct use of *Basic Concepts in Music* will certainly leave more time for actual involvement with music, and will foster a continuing positive attitude in class.

I wish to thank the following reviewers for their helpful comments and suggestions: John F. Fisher, University of Iowa; David Liptak, Michigan State University; Russell Nelson, Lock Haven State College; and William Triplett, University of Southern California.

Gary M. Martin

Introduction

1

Programmed learning may be a new experience for you. This book is called a "scrambled" or "branching" program because the book cannot be read by turning consecutive pages. The book is divided into frames or small numbered units of instruction. You will frequently find two or three such numbers on one page. Depending on your mastery of certain principles, you may skip many frames of the book. For example, from frame 26 you may be instructed to turn to frame 31 to continue reading. Therefore, when you finish reading each frame, it is important to note where you read next.

At the end of each chapter are two features that will be of great value to you in your study. The first, *Skill Builders*, will help you translate musical concepts into usable skills. The second, *Self-Tests*, will help you discover the chapter topics you have mastered and the ones you need to review.

You have reached the end of frame 1. Please turn to frame 3.

2

Oops!!

You did not follow instructions but fell into the habit of reading pages in consecutive order. You cannot do this in a programmed textbook. Please return to frame 1 and follow the directions.

3

Good. You have followed the first instruction encountered in your study.

On certain pages, you will see the caption *Use the Shield*. When so directed, you should use the shield (attached inside the front cover of the book) to conceal the page below the part you are reading. Complete instructions for its use are printed on the shield.

At frequent intervals in the book, *Diagnostic Questions* will test your knowledge of some musical concept. To the right of each possible answer will be a frame number. Select the answer you think is right and turn to the frame indicated. There you will find whether or not your answer was correct. If it was correct, a new Diagnostic Question will be presented. If your answer was incorrect, an explanation will follow. If you are unsure of the answer or realize your answer would be a guess, choose the alternative "I'm unsure" (or one similarly worded). You will then be directed to a detailed discussion of the subject. Remember, your basic purpose in reading this book is to gain an understanding of the fundamentals of music. Honesty about what you know and don't know is imperative, and guessing will serve no useful purpose.

When you miss a question, you may be asked to reread certain frames. Be sure to read them even more carefully the second time, for you will probably meet the question again to test your adjustment since the initial mistake.

Because musical concepts build on each other, a secure knowledge of each topic is essential to understanding the next. Therefore, at the end of each chapter a *Self-Test* will help you determine what you have learned—and whether or not you are ready to go on to the next chapter. You will also have a chance to review any material that still confuses you.

It is hoped that this book will be an interesting and informative experience for you. Go to frame 4.

1
Basic Components of Music Notation

A musical sound is a fleeting experience. To retain musical sounds for future reproduction, a system of notation was developed, just as a system of writing was developed to record the spoken word. This chapter deals with the basic symbols and words that constitute the modern music notational system. Chapter 1 contains seven Diagnostic Questions.

Objectives

After completing this chapter, you should be able to identify correctly the following musical terms and their equivalent symbols.

1. A music staff, the grand staff, and ledger lines.
2. The treble clef and bass clef signs.
3. A bar line and a measure.
4. Whole, half, quarter, eighth, and sixteenth notes.
5. Whole, half, quarter, eighth, and sixteenth rests.
6. The highest and lowest notes in a musical passage.

You should also be able to identify the action specified by each of the following words or symbols that are used in musical notation.

1. Crescendo
2. Decrescendo
3. D.C. (da capo)
4. D.S. (dal segno)
5. Fine
6. Repeat sign: ‖: :‖

Finally, you should be able to write musical notes on staff paper following established rules of musical calligraphy.

Now go to frame 5.

Diagnostic Question One

In the example below are some musical symbols, numbered 1–6. Choose the alternative that correctly matches the numbered symbol with its name.

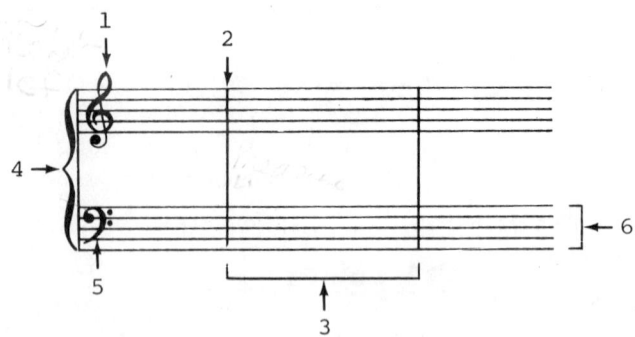

Alternatives

			frame
a.	I am unsure. Please explain this.		6
b.	1 — treble clef sign 2 — bar line 3 — measure	4 — grand staff 5 — bass clef sign 6 — staff lines	13
c.	1 — bass clef sign 2 — bar line 3 — measure	4 — grand staff 5 — treble clef sign 6 — staff lines	19
d.	1 — treble clef sign 2 — measure 3 — bar line	4 — staff lines 5 — bass clef sign 6 — grand staff	15

You have helped yourself by stating frankly that you are not familiar with some of these musical symbols, and the following discussion will help you identify them.

Five lines placed together, as shown on the right, form a *staff*.

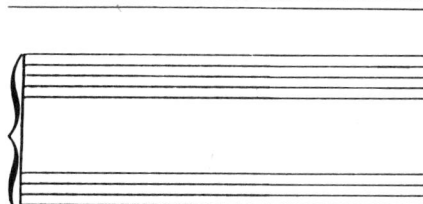

When two staves are used together they are called the *grand staff*.

On the grand staff, special signs are used to designate the top staff, called the *treble clef*,

and bottom staff, called the *bass clef*. The sign for the top staff looks like this: It is called the *treble clef sign*.

Perhaps you know that a male singer with a very low voice is called a *bass*. The sign for the bottom staff, the *bass clef sign*, looks like this: 𝄢 .

Complete the following statements.

Use the Shield.

When we use these signs in music notation we have a _____ staff with treble clef and bass clef signs.

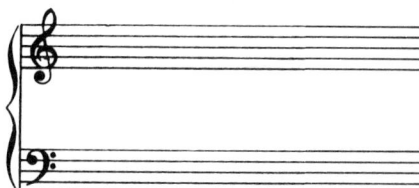

☙

grand

The sign for the bottom staff is the _____ clef sign.

☙

bass

The _____ clef sign identifies the top staff.

☙

treble

Go to frame 7.

7

Use the Shield.

This notation 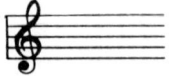 is called the _____ clef.

treble

The treble clef is the top staff, and the bottom staff is the _____ clef.

bass

When the treble clef and the bass clef are joined together, we have an example of the _____.

grand staff

Put the Shield Aside.

The staff can be divided into sections with vertical lines called *bar lines*. The distance between any two bar lines is called a *measure*.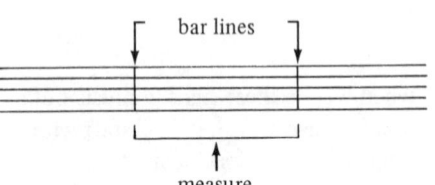

In the example below, there are three bar lines and two measures.

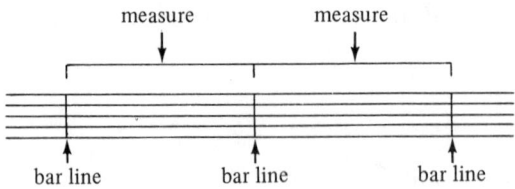

Turn to frame 8.

8

Use the Shield.

This distance ⊟ is called a _____ .

☙

measure

A measure is the distance between two _____ _____ .

☙

bar lines

Bar lines are drawn on 5 lines known as the musical _____ .

☙

staff

Put the Shield Aside.

Fill in the blank spaces below to identify correctly each of the notational symbols shown. Then check your answers with the key in frame 12.

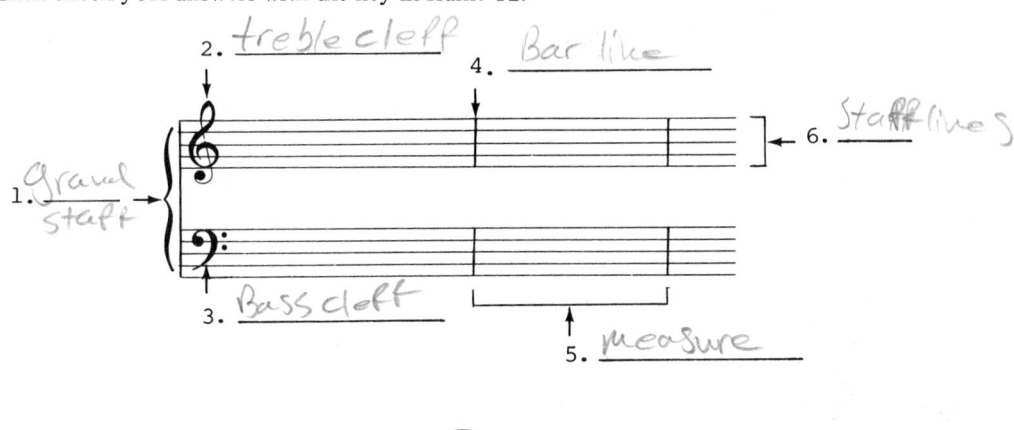

9

That example tripped you up. To find out why, turn to frame 14.

10

The alternative you selected contained an error.

Let's look at those notes again:

    𝐨 — Whole note.

    𝅗𝅥 — Add a stem and you get a half note.

    ♩ — Fill in the note and it becomes a quarter note.

    ♪ — Put a flag on it and it is an eighth note.

    𝅘𝅥𝅯 — Put two flags on it and it is called a sixteenth note.

If you were to add still another flag, what would you have then? Of course, you would have a thirty-second note.

For further instruction, turn to frame 21. If you are ready to answer the Diagnostic Question, turn to frame 16.

11

Congratulations, you have correctly identified whole, half, quarter, eighth, and sixteenth notes. Turn to frame 24.

Notation Symbols:

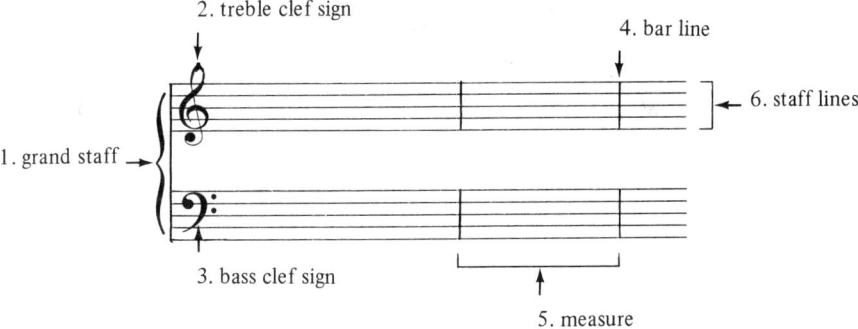

Now return to frame 5 and answer the Diagnostic Question.

Right! The names of the musical symbols are given below. I'm glad you have identified them.

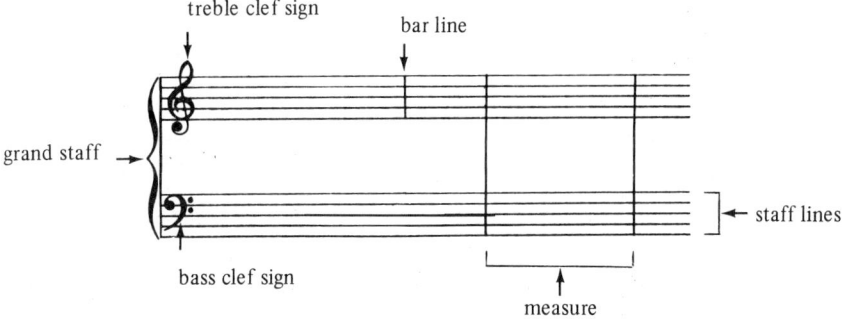

Having demonstrated that you know the basic framework for musical notation, you are ready to consider the notation of musical rhythm.

Go to frame 16.

14

It will take only a short time to learn these note values. In music, the notes are assigned the arithmetic values of whole (1/1), half (1/2), quarter (1/4), eighth (1/8), and sixteenth (1/16). The symbols for these notes are simply and logically constructed.

1. An elliptical circle is a *whole* note: 𝒐
2. Put a stem on the whole note and it becomes a *half* note: 𝅗𝅥
3. Fill in the half note and it becomes a *quarter* note: ♩
4. Put a flag on the stem of the quarter note and it becomes an *eighth* note: ♪
5. Put a second flag on the stem of the eighth note and it becomes a *sixteenth* note: 𝅘𝅥𝅯

We now have the following symbols:

𝒐 = whole note   ♪ = eighth note

𝅗𝅥 = half note   𝅘𝅥𝅯 = sixteenth note

♩ = quarter note

The duration of the whole note (𝒐) is four times as long as the duration of the quarter note (♩). The time value of the whole note is therefore four times as great as the time value of the quarter note.

Now turn to frame 21.

15

There seems to be something about this example that confuses you. By selecting this alternative, you indicated that you must have known something about music, or you would have chosen the alternative "I'm unsure." For an explanation of the six basic symbols, turn to frame 19.

16

Diagnostic Question Two

To refer to the relative duration of musical notes, we will use the term *time value*. A note's time value indicates how long it is held in relation to other notes. The most common time values are represented by the whole note, half note, quarter note, eighth note, and sixteenth note, which are shown below. You must identify them. Again, there are four alternative responses. After choosing your alternative, turn to the appropriate frame.

Alternatives

			frame
a.	I'm not familiar with these time values.		14
b.	1 — eighth note 2 — quarter note 3 — whole note	4 — half note 5 — sixteenth note	10
c.	1 — sixteenth note 2 — eighth note 3 — whole note	4 — half note 5 — quarter note	9
d.	1 — sixteenth note 2 — quarter note 3 — whole note	4 — half note 5 — eighth note	11

17

Instead of an equal pair, you chose an unequal pair: the quarter note ♩ and the eighth rest ♪ . For an explanation go to frame 28.

18

Complete the following exercise by filling in the blanks:

Use the Shield.

This ▬ is a _____ rest.

🙵

half

This 𝟩 is a(n) _____ rest.

🙵

eighth

This 𝄽 is a _____ rest.

🙵

quarter

The whole rest is written (*above/below*) the line.

🙵

below

This ▬ is a _____ rest.

🙵

whole

The two rests 𝄽 and 𝟩 are _____ and _____ rests.

🙵

quarter, eighth

Of the rests 𝄽 , 𝟩 , and 𝟩 , which has the *greatest* time value?

🙵

quarter rest (𝄽)

Go to frame 31.

19

You identified some of the symbols correctly, but others incorrectly.

Five horizontal lines placed together are called the *staff* or *staff lines*.

When two staves are placed together, they are called the *grand staff*.

Special symbols are used on the grand staff to differentiate the top staff, or *treble clef*, from the bottom staff, or *bass clef*.

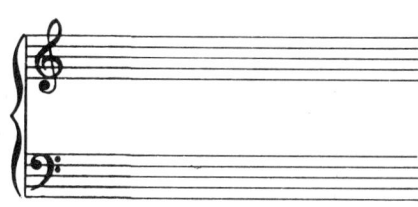

The grand staff is divided into sections by *bar lines*. The distance between two bar lines is called a *measure*.

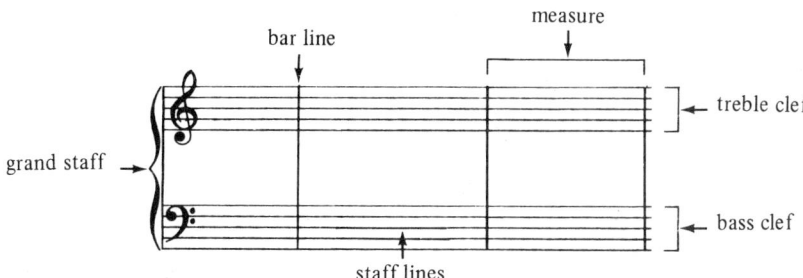

Return to the Diagnostic Question in frame 5 and see if you can now answer it correctly.

20

You were asked to choose a pair equal in time value, but you chose the eighth note (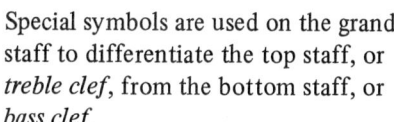) and whole rest ( ), which are incorrectly matched. For a review of this question, turn to frame 28.

Answer the following questions:

Use the Shield.

This (o) is called a _____ note.

⇃§
whole

The whole note has the (*longest/ shortest*) time value of the notes on the right.

o 𝅗𝅥 ♩ ♪ 𝅘𝅥𝅯

⇃§
longest

The note with the shortest time value in the above example would be the _____ note.

⇃§
sixteenth

How many quarter notes does it take to equal one half note?

⇃§
two

Put the Shield Aside.

Write the words whole, half, quarter, eighth, and sixteenth under the appropriate notes. If you need a review, see frame 14.

𝅗𝅥   ♪   ♩   𝅘𝅥𝅯   o

<u>half</u>   <u>eighth</u>   <u>quarter</u>   <u>sixteenth</u>   <u>whole</u>

Now return to frame 16 and see if you can answer the Diagnostic Question correctly.

22

Just follow this one very simple rule: *The higher the note is on the staff, the higher it is in sound; the lower the note is on the staff, the lower it is in sound.*

On the grand staff, the pitches of the bass clef are lower than the pitches of the treble clef. When music becomes too low to be written conveniently on the treble staff, it is written on the bass staff. The illustration above is a good example of a melody using both staves.

Notes are written on staff *lines* and in the *spaces* between the lines. Notes very close to each other in pitch may appear on adjacent lines and spaces, a fact that demands careful observation by the inexperienced reader. Several examples of such adjacent notes are shown below.

Now carefully find the highest and lowest notes in the Diagnostic Question in frame 34.

23

Not quite. It is easy to become confused about foreign words, as you just have. For an explanation that will help you remember them, read frame 36.

24

Diagnostic Question Three

There are times in music when a brief silence, or a *rest*, is desirable. The symbols for the time values of rests are comparable to notes; there are whole, half, quarter, eighth, and sixteenth rests. The whole rest is equal in time value to the whole note; the half rest is equal to the half note, and so on.

In the example below, notes are paired with rests. All pairs except one match symbols of unequal time value. Find the *equal* pair and turn to the designated frame. (If you need a review of note values, turn to frame 21.)

Alternatives

		frame
a.	I'm not sure I know the symbols for rests. Please explain them to me.	28
b.	♩ = 𝄾	17
c.	♪ = ▬	20
d.	○ = ▪	29
e.	𝅝 = 𝄽	33

25

That alternative is wrong. Be sure that wasn't just a guess. Please read frame 22.

26

Good. You are now ready to learn the meanings of musical directions that appear at the edge of the staff.

Diagnostic Question Four

Match the musical directions in column 1 with their proper descriptions in column 2.

1. D.S. (*dal segno*)
2. D.C. (*da capo*)
3. Fine
4. ‖: :‖

A. go to the sign
B. the end
C. repeat sign
D. go to the beginning

Alternatives

			frame
a.	I'm not sure. Please explain.		36
b.	1 = A 2 = D	3 = C 4 = B	35
c.	1 = A 2 = D	3 = B 4 = C	32
d.	1 = D 2 = A	3 = B 4 = C	23

27

Very good! Hang on now, you have almost finished the chapter. Turn to frame 40.

28

Once you know the time values of notes, the time values of musical rests are easy to learn.

The *whole* rest carries the largest time value, and the *half* rest the second largest. These two rests look very much alike, as you can see in the example below.

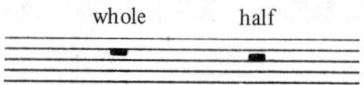

Here is a simple device to keep them from confusing you:

1. A whole rest (▬) is larger than a half rest in time value. Because it is larger (and therefore heavier), it hangs *below* the staff line.
2. The half rest (▬) has a smaller time value than the whole rest. Because it is smaller (and therefore lighter), it sits *on top of* the staff line.

The next symbol (𝄽) is a quarter rest. Look at its shape carefully. The final symbols you need to recognize are the eighth and sixteenth rests. The eighth rest looks like this: 𝄾 . To make a sixteenth rest, just add another flag to the stem of the eighth rest: 𝄿 .

Can you guess how to make a thirty-second rest? Yes, just add another flag to the stem.

Thirty-second rest: 𝅀 .

To review briefly:

▬ = whole rest (below the line)
▬ = half rest (above the line)
𝄽 = quarter rest
𝄾 = eighth rest
𝄿 = sixteenth rest

Go to frame 18.

29

Right! You are now ready to consider pitch determination. For that, turn to frame 34.

30

Put the Shield Aside.

Let's add the words together now:

1. *D.C. al fine* means: go to the beginning and play to the word "fine."
2. *D.S. al fine* means: return to the sign 𝄋 and play to the word "fine."
3. Although it isn't Italian, you must also remember this symbol:

𝄆 𝄇 (repeat sign). The arrows below show where to go when you see a repeat sign.

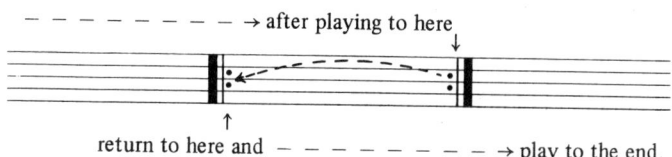

Use the Shield.

D.S. al fine means to go to _____ .

⋕

the sign and play to the end.

This sign 𝄆 𝄇 means that I should repeat the music that is found (*before/between/after*) the double bars.

⋕

between

D.C. stands for which Italian words?

⋕

Da Capo

Bene, ora parla un poco Italiano (which means, "Good, now you speak a little Italian").

Now, return to frame 26 and answer the Diagnostic Question.

31

Use the Shield.

In the example on the right, only the __________ rest is correctly marked.

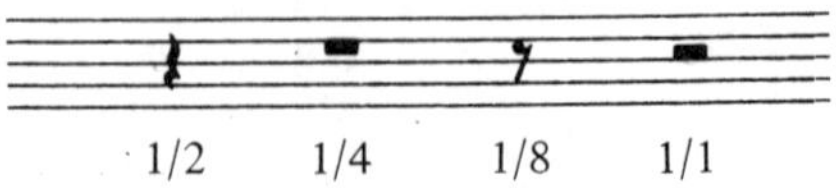

𝄾 = *1/8*

How many rests are correctly labeled?

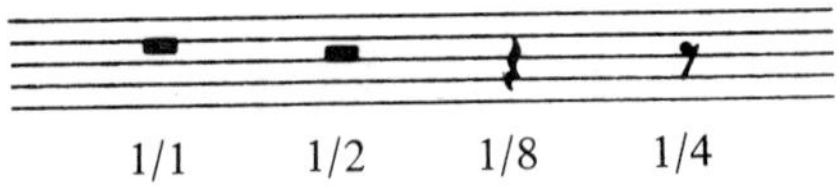

two: 𝄻 = *1/1;* 𝄼 = *1/2*

If you made mistakes on this frame or frame 19, review the rest symbols again, beginning with frame 28. If you made no mistakes, return to frame 24 and answer the Diagnostic Question.

32

Molto bene! (That's Italian for "very good.") Now try another matching question, this time using dynamic markings, in frame 37.

33

You were asked to choose a pair equal in time value, but you chose an unequal pair: the whole note (𝅝) and the quarter rest (𝄽). Please go to frame 28.

34

Diagnostic Question Five

Music is composed of notes that vary in pitch from low to high. Do you know how to distinguish the lower notes from the higher ones on the written page? From the example below, choose the alternative that identifies the *highest* and the *lowest* notes in the whole example, in that order.

Alternatives

				frame
a.	I'm not sure.			22
	High	Low		
b.	1	and	8	25
c.	1	and	5	38
d.	2	and	5	26

35

No, you have confused the repeat sign with the word *fine*, which is the Italian counterpart of our word finish or *end*. Go to frame 36.

36

If you understand the meanings of the Italian words, it will help you remember how they are used in musical context. D.S. are the initials for the Italian words *dal segno* (pronounced "doll *sane*-yo"), which mean *from the sign*. The sign referred to looks like this: _____. When you see D.S., you are supposed to *go back to the sign* (𝄋) and begin playing from that point, thereby repeating the passage.

The second symbol was D.C., initials for the Italian words *da capo* (pronounced "dah *cop*-oh"). "Capo" is related to our English word "head" or "beginning." In music it means *go back to the top* or *go back to the beginning*.

D.S. = go to the sign
D.C. = go to the beginning

The Italian word *fine* (pronounced "*fee*-nay") is related to the English word "finish." It means simply *stop here* or *the end*.

Now fill in the blanks to complete the sentences below:

Use the Shield.

If I were playing a piece of music on the piano and I came to the initials D.S. I would go back to the _____ and play from there.

☙

sign: 𝄋

If I came to the initials D.C. I would go back to the _____.

☙

beginning

The initials ____ ____ instruct me to return to this sign 𝄋 and play from there.

☙

D.S.

Turn to frame 30.

37

Diagnostic Question Six

Dynamic markings determine how loud or soft the music should be. Dynamics in music are indicated by Italian abbreviations.

p = soft   f = loud   m = medium

Below are two columns. Match the dynamic markings on the left with the proper definition from the column on the right and select the correct alternative.

Markings	Definitions
1. pp (pianissimo) E	A. loud
2. ff (fortissimo) C	B. soft
3. p (piano) B	C. very loud
4. f (forte) A	D. medium soft
5. mp (mezzo piano) D	E. very soft

Alternatives

		frame
a.	I'm not sure. Where is the explanation?	39
b.	1 = E 4 = A 2 = C 5 = B 3 = D	42
c.	1 = E 4 = A 2 = C 5 = D 3 = B	27
d.	1 = C 4 = A 2 = D 5 = E 3 = B	41

38

No. You are right about the lowest note, but your choice for the highest note was wrong. Go to frame 22.

39

All of the abbreviations p, pp, mp, f, ff, and mf refer to various degrees of loudness or softness of musical tone. If you can remember the meanings of just three letters, the dynamic markings will be easy to understand.

p – *soft*   f – *loud*   m – *medium*

So, if you have two "f's" (ff), the symbol would mean doubly loud or better, *very loud*. Two "p's" (pp) would mean doubly soft or better, *very soft*. An "m" in front of either denotes moderation. Thus, "mp" means moderately soft, and "mf" means moderately loud.

Progressing from the softest sound on the left to the loudest sound on the right, we have the following series of symbols:

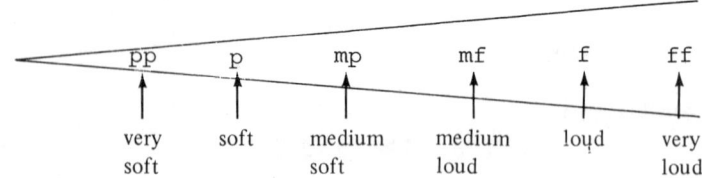

Do the following exercise:

Use the Shield.

The softest sound in music would be identified by using the letter _____ several times in a row.

p

Ranging from softest to loudest sounds, which of the following symbols are *not* in the correct order?

(softest)   pp   p   mf   mp   f   ff   (loudest)

mf and mp are reversed.

Now return to frame 37 and answer the Diagnostic Question.

===== 40 =====

Diagnostic Question Seven

Do you know the meanings of the terms crescendo and decrescendo and their accompanying symbols, ? One of them means to become softer, and the other means to become louder. The following statements are either true or false:

1. Crescendo means to become louder.
2. Decrescendo means to become softer.

Alternatives

	frame
a. Both statements are true.	44
b. Both statements are false.	43

===== 41 =====

You have made a mistake, but the following explanation should help you understand these symbols. Read on in frame 39.

===== 42 =====

You've confused two of the symbols. The explanation that should clear up the problem for you is in frame 39.

No, that was not the correct alternative. A look at the chart below should clarify the problem.

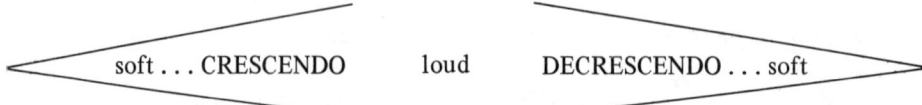

Crescendo means *to become louder*, and decrescendo means *to become softer*. Decrescendo has the same prefix (de-) as decrease, and the word means *to decrease in volume of sound*.

Turn back to frame 40 and see if you can answer the Diagnostic Question.

Correct. The prefix "de-" on decrescendo means to decrease the sound.

It is now time to develop the ability to write these musical symbols yourself. To learn how, turn to frame 45.

MUSICAL CALLIGRAPHY

When a person begins to write music, it most frequently looks very strange (and is difficult to read) unless several rules are observed. Some of the more important ones are introduced here in four groups.

Group A: Writing Individual Notes (5 Rules)

RULE 1: Notes are not to be drawn as circles. They are *oval* in shape, and are tilted slightly *away* from the stem.

RULE 2: If the note stem goes up, it is drawn on the *right* side of the note. If the note stem goes down, it is drawn on the *left* side.

RULE 3: The note stem is normally drawn toward the center of the staff rather than toward the top or bottom edge of the staff.

RULE 4: A note stem should normally be 3 lines or 3 spaces long, but should never end on a staff line.

Turn to frame 46.

RULE 5: The note stem should always be drawn at a right angle to the staff lines. Flags on note stems taper smoothly into the stem.

incorrect   correct

Group B: Writing Groups of Notes (4 Rules)

RULE 6: When writing notes of shorter rhythmic duration than a quarter note, *flags* and *beams* are equivalent, and may be used interchangeably without affecting time values.

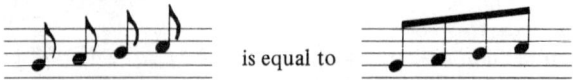

RULE 7: Beams are *not* to be placed across bar lines.

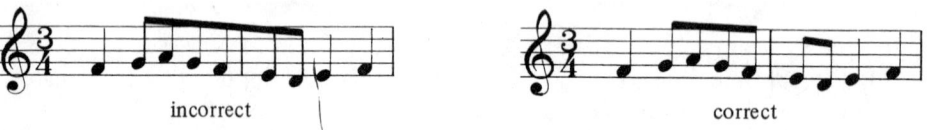

incorrect   correct

RULE 8:* Beams may be substituted for flags only if *complete beats* are involved.

incorrect   correct

NOTE: You have not received sufficient information to understand fully rules 8 and 9 at this stage of the program. They are presented here because they are part of Group B calligraphy, and they will need your attention later.

Turn to frame 47.

RULE 9:* The space in any given measure is equally divided into beats, and notes are to be written in the appropriate spaces.

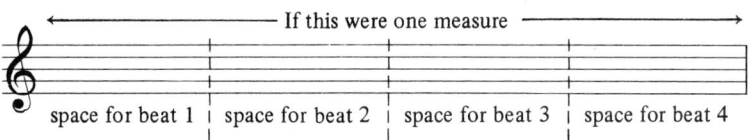

incorrect

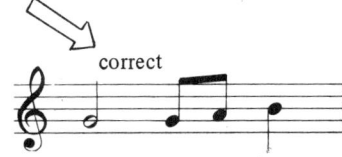

correct

All notes are equally spaced. The half note should fill the space for the first *two* beats, the two eighths combined fill the third space, and the quarter note fills the last space.

Group C: Writing Sharps, Flats, Naturals, and Clef Signs

RULE 10: Sharps, flats, and naturals are written in front of the note they affect.

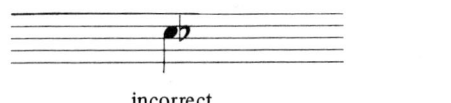

incorrect

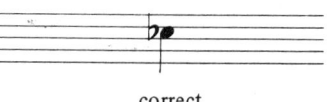

correct

RULE 11: Sharps consist of two long, thin lines (perpendicular) and two short, thick lines (slightly off horizontal) that surround the line or space to be sharped.

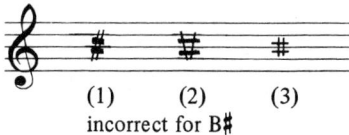

(1) (2) (3)
incorrect for B♯

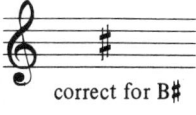

correct for B♯

Turn to frame 48.

RULE 12: Flats consist of a stem and the right half of a heart-like figure (♭) that surrounds the line or space to be flatted.

(1) (2)
incorrect

correct

RULE 13: Natural signs are made in two steps (shown below), and form a box around the note they affect.

Step 1:

Step 2:

RULE 14: The treble clef (or 𝄞 clef) sign is made in three steps. It crosses the staff line for G *four* times. (It is sometimes called the G clef because of this use to designate the note G. Its shape was originally that of a script G.)

G →   Step 1   Step 2   G →   Step 3

RULE 15: The bass clef (or 𝄢 clef) sign is made in two steps. The dots are placed around the second line from the top to designate that line as F. (The sign was once a script F.)

Step 1

F
↓
x

Step 2

Group D: Writing Rests

RULE 16: Whole rests hang from the middle line and fill one-half of the space below.

(1)   (2)   (3)
incorrect

correct

Turn to frame 49.

RULE 17: Half rests sit on the middle line and fill one-half of the space above the line.

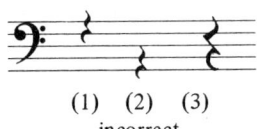
(1)   (2)   (3)
incorrect

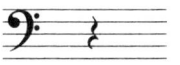
correct

RULE 18: Quarter rests cover the middle two-thirds of the staff, and consist of three characters:
(a) an open C, inverted,
(b) a short, straight line,
(c) an open C.

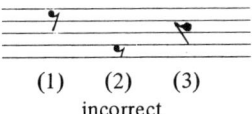
(1)   (2)   (3)
incorrect

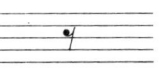
correct

RULE 19: Eighth rests somewhat resemble a percentage sign without the bottom dot (𝄾), and cover about one-half of the middle of the staff.

(1)   (2)   (3)
incorrect

correct

RULE 20: Sixteenth rests are similar to eighth rests with an extended stem and added tail.

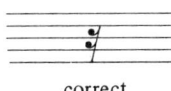
correct

Turn to frame 50.

50

Now write each of the following musical symbols on the staff lines provided on the right.

1. INDIVIDUAL NOTES

2. GROUPS OF NOTES

3. SHARPS, FLATS, NATURALS, AND CLEF SIGNS

4. RESTS

Here are other staff lines. Practice writing any symbols that need further attention.

Turn to the next frame.

51

♦ **THE NEXT STEP...**

At several points in the book you will find brief sections designated THE NEXT STEP.... Such sections introduce material beyond the scope of the chapter, and are for your information if you desire it. You may, however, skip this section if you wish.

Double whole notes and thirty-second notes: If you want to hold a tone for twice as long as indicated by a whole note, the double whole note is used. Likewise thirty-second notes (and even sixty-fourth notes) may be seen, although infrequently.

♦   double whole note   thirty-second note   sixty-fourth note

You have now completed the first chapter. The next step is to refine your abilities by completing the following activities.

Skill Builders

1. Clap the rhythm of the song "This Old Man" (frame 52) by reading the notes and clapping the rhythm you see. Be sure to observe the rests.

2. Sing the melody of "This Old Man," using the words "long" or "ta" for quarter notes, and "short" or "te" for eighth notes.

3. Identify by name all the printed symbols in the song, including the time values of the notes and rests.

Turn to frame 52.

52

THIS OLD MAN

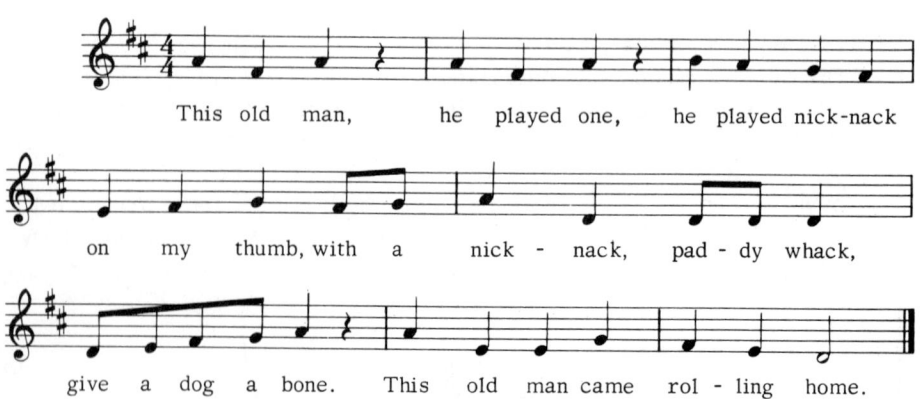

This old man, he played one, he played nick-nack on my thumb, with a nick-nack, pad-dy whack, give a dog a bone. This old man came rol-ling home.

Verse 2:	on my shoe.	Verse 7:	up in heaven.
Verse 3:	on my knee.	Verse 8:	on the gate.
Verse 4:	on my door.	Verse 9:	on my spine.
Verse 5:	on my hive.	Verse 10:	once again.
Verse 6:	on my sticks.		

4. Copy the song "This Old Man" on the blank staff lines below. Some common errors to watch out for include (a) putting the stem on the wrong side of the note, (b) failing to write notes squarely on the line or in the space, and (c) crowding the notes together, making them difficult to read.

Turn to frame 53.

5. Identify the highest and lowest notes in both songs below. Then chant each of the songs twice, first using the words of the songs, then using "long" or "ta" for quarter notes and "short" or "te" for eighth notes. Try singing all the songs you have worked with in this chapter.

GO TELL AUNT RHODY

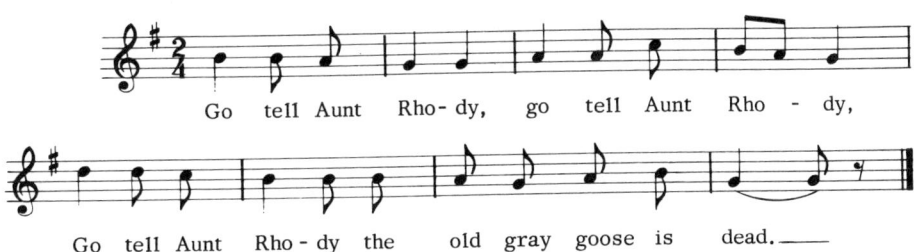

Verse 2: The one she's been saving (repeat two times) to make a feather bed.
Verse 3: The goslings are crying (repeat two times) because the goose is dead.
Verse 4: The gander is grieving (repeat two times) because the goose is dead.

BINGO

Turn to frame 54.

Self-Test

On the left is a column of musical symbols and numbered blanks. At the right is a list of their names. Match each symbol with its correct name, and record the proper letter in the blank.

1. ____

2. ____

3. ____

4. ____

5. ____

6. ____

A. bass clef
B. bar line
C. grand staff
D. measure
E. staff lines
F. treble clef

7. Arrange the following symbols in the order necessary to create a decrescendo.

    p   f   mp   mf   pp

8. Identify each of the notes *and* rests in "Old MacDonald Had a Farm" (frame 55) as a whole, half, quarter, or eighth by writing the first letter of that word next to the note (that is, q = quarter, h = half, and so on).

9. Describe what the D.C. al fine at the end of the fourth line of the song instructs you to do. _____.

10. Circle the song's highest and lowest notes.

11. How many measures are there in the song?

Please turn to frame 55.

OLD MACDONALD HAD A FARM

folk tune

1. Old Mac-Don-ald had a farm, E-I-E-I-

O! And on this farm he had some chicks,

E-I-E-I-O! With a chick, chick here and a

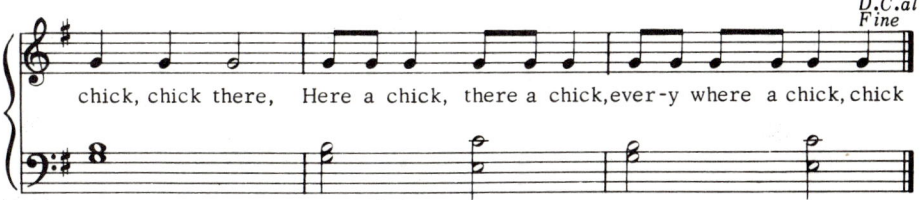
chick, chick there, Here a chick, there a chick, ev-ry where a chick, chick

Verse 2:   Duck: quack, quack.
Verse 3:   Pig: oink, oink.
Verse 4:   Dog: bow, wow, etc.

Turn to frame 56.

Write the following musical symbols on the staff below.

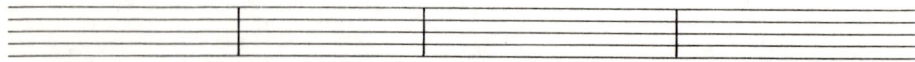

    12. quarter rest   13. sixteenth note on   14. treble clef sign   15. sharp sign on
                                            bottom line   middle line

Write the following musical symbols on the staff below.

    16. flat on middle line   17. bass clef sign   18. half note on top line   19. whole rest

20.   Write two eighth notes in each measure at the right. Write them in the following manner: (1) first measure = one on the top line and one on the second line; (b) second measure = one on the third line and one of the fourth line; (c) use beams, not flags.

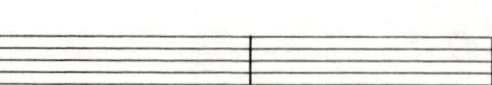

Now check your answers with those in the answer key (frame 57) and grade your results. If you missed a substantial number of items, you need a review of the chapter. (You should be able to finish it much faster the second time.) Regardless of your grade, *if you missed any questions*, it is important to review them immediately. The number of the frame where you can review a missed question is shown next to the answer.

Turn to frame 57.

Answers & Review Index

Beside each answer, the topic and frame number are shown in parentheses.

1. E (staff lines, 6)
2. F (treble clef, 6)
3. C (grand staff, 6)
4. A (bass clef, 6)
5. B (bar line, 7)
6. D (measure, 7)
7. f mf mp p pp   (dynamic levels, 39)

8. line 1, treble clef: q q q q q q h, q q q q
   line 1, bass clef: h h h h h

   line 2, treble clef: h! (q) q q q q q q h
   line 2, bass clef: h q (q) h h h h

   line 3, treble clef: q q q q h (q) e e q q q e e
   line 3, bass clef: h h h (h) w

   line 4, treble clef: q q h e e q e e q e e e e q q
   line 4, bass clef: w h h h h   (rhythmic values, 14)

9. D.C. al fine means: Go back to the beginning of the song, and sing to the beginning of the second line, E-I-E-I-O! (D.C., 36)

10. Highest note: the notes above *E-I*.
    Lowest note: line 2, bass clef, the quarter note under *-O!*   (pitch, 22)

11. Twelve measures are printed. There are sixteen measures if you count the D.C. al fine measures twice. (measure, 7)

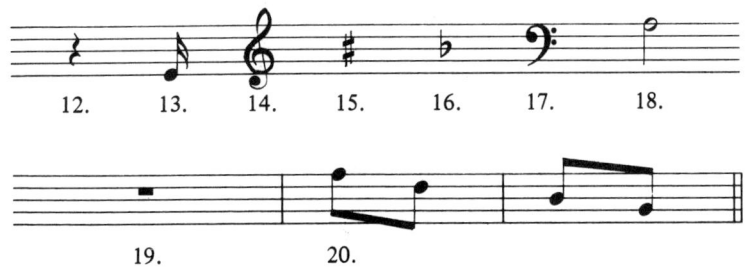

(Items 12–20, review frames 45–49)

Now review all questions missed. Then turn to Chapter 2 (frame 58).

2
Basic Components of Rhythm

58

Three of the most important components of music are rhythm, melody, and harmony. This chapter is primarily concerned with rhythm.

In the preceding chapter, you learned to identify whole, half, quarter, eighth, and sixteenth notes and rests. You are now going to apply your understanding of time values to more complex rhythmic concepts. Read the objectives carefully for a full understanding of what will be required of you at the end of the chapter. This chapter has 11 Diagnostic Questions.

Objectives

When you reach the end of Chapter 2, you will be asked to do the following:

1. Distinguish between definitions of rhythm, pulse, meter, and tempo.
2. Identify various meter (time) signatures used in music.
3. Illustrate the number of notes and the kinds of notes called for in each of the meter signatures.
4. Match measures of music with their appropriate meter signatures.
5. Identify some of the various rhythmic possibilities in a measure of music.
6. Distinguish between simple and compound meters.

Most of these items relate to meter signatures and their use. You will also be asked to identify these rhythmic features of music:

1. Two ways of writing eighth and sixteenth notes.
2. Tied notes and dotted notes, and the changes in note duration they indicate.
3. Accents, tenuto and staccato marks, pickup notes, and slurred notes.

It is good that you took the time to read the objectives. We seem to learn better when it is clear what is expected of us. Turn to frame 59.

In its broadest sense, rhythm has been defined as "the aspect of music that relates to forward movement." It may be more simply called a "progression of musical sounds through time." Anyone who has danced or even tapped a foot to music has experienced this feeling of movement through time, or as it is better known, rhythm.

Some words that relate to the concept of rhythm are pulse, meter, and tempo. In the following question, match the terms with the appropriate definitions.

Diagnostic Question One

Terms

A. rhythm
B. pulse
C. meter
D. tempo

Definitions

1. Regularly spaced beats in music. The underlying steady beat in music.

2. The rate of movement (e.g. slow or fast) in music.

3. The organization of beats into groups of two, three or more. Usually repeated consistently and identifiably.

4. The progression of musical sounds through time.

Alternatives

		frame
1.	A-4, B-2, C-1, D-3	71
2.	A-4, B-3, C-2, D-1	65
3.	A-4, B-1, C-3, D-2	64

60

You must have overlooked something. Please turn to frame 66 for an explanation.

61

That wasn't a poor guess, was it? Let's explore the answer.

The question was: What two notes does this note (♩·) equal? The dotted quarter note (♩·) is equal to one and one-half the value of a quarter note. If that tip is sufficient for you to answer the Diagnostic Question correctly, return to frame 72. A more detailed review begins in frame 73.

62

Not quite. Here's hoping that wasn't just a guess. The question was:

What two notes does this note (♩·) equal? It is a dotted quarter note, and remember, *a dot after a note always increases the duration of the note by one-half of that note's value.* If you are ready to try the question again, return to frame 72. A more detailed review begins in frame 73.

Diagnostic Question Two

Which of the following musical equations is correct throughout?

Alternatives

                                                                                                    frame

a.   I'm not really sure which is right.
      May I review this concept?   66

b. 𝅗𝅥 = 𝅘𝅥 𝅘𝅥 = 𝅘𝅥𝅮 𝅘𝅥𝅮 𝅘𝅥𝅮 𝅘𝅥𝅮 or 𝅘𝅥𝅮𝅘𝅥𝅮𝅘𝅥𝅮𝅘𝅥𝅮 𝅘𝅥𝅮𝅘𝅥𝅮𝅘𝅥𝅮𝅘𝅥𝅮   70

c. 𝅗𝅥 = 𝅘𝅥 𝅘𝅥 = 𝅘𝅥𝅮 𝅘𝅥𝅮 or 𝅘𝅥𝅮𝅘𝅥𝅮   68

d. 𝅗𝅥 = 𝅘𝅥 𝅘𝅥 = 𝅘𝅥𝅮 𝅘𝅥𝅮 𝅘𝅥𝅮 𝅘𝅥𝅮   76

You are right. The four terms may be defined as follows:

Rhythm: the progression of musical sounds through time.
Pulse: regularly spaced beats in music.
Tempo: rate of movement in music.
Meter: organization of beats into groups of two, three, or more.

Diagnostic Question Three

The mathematical relationship of music notes is illustrated on the right. Observe the two ways of writing eighth and sixteenth notes shown in the chart—with flags or with connecting beams. There is absolutely no difference in time value between the two ways of writing eighth notes.

Which of the following musical equations is mathematically correct?

Alternatives

		frame
a.	I prefer a review of these note values.	66
b.	o = ♩♩ = ♪♪♪♪	74
c.	o = ♩♩ = ♪♪♪♪	69
d.	o = ♩♩ = ♪♪♪♪	60

That isn't quite right. Here is a brief discussion of each term.

RHYTHM: Music exists in time. Each sound we hear moves us forward in the musical experience. The generic term for all such movement in sound is *rhythm*. Many other terms have to do with some aspect of rhythm, but none of them are as all-encompassing as is rhythm itself. It is commonly identified as one of the elements of music.

PULSE: When sounds occur in music they may occur at fixed, equal intervals of time, or they may occur at unpredictable intervals. If they occur at equal intervals, they are known as *pulse* (much like the pulse of a heart beat). It is common to have an underlying pulse in music with elaborate rhythmic patterns of many kinds occurring at the same time.

TEMPO: When musical sounds occur, they follow one another at a given rate, or speed. The term used to designate this rate of movement is *tempo*.

METER: As was stated above, pulse is very commonly found in music. It does not usually exist, however, as pure pulse. Rather, the beats are organized into groups of two, three, or more. The first beat of each group usually receives a slight stress, making the group audible as a unit: *one* - two - three, *one* - two - three. The grouping of pulses into units is known as *meter*.

Now return to frame 59 and answer the question.

First, let's look at the individual notes under consideration:

𝐨 = whole note   ♩ = quarter note

𝅗𝅥 = half note   ♪ = eighth note

As you learned in arithmetic, it takes two eighths to equal one fourth. Similarly in music, two eighths equal one fourth—or one quarter note: ♪♪ = ♩ ; two fourths equal one half: ♩ ♩ = 𝅗𝅥 ; and two halves equal one whole: 𝅗𝅥 𝅗𝅥 = 𝐨 . Therefore,

1 whole = 2 halves = 4 quarters = 8 eighths

You can change the order of these notes, or you can leave out an entire group between the equal signs, but you may not leave out any part of a group.

Correct ♩ ♩ = 𝐨 = ♩ ♩ ♩ ♩

Incorrect ♩ = 𝐨 = ♩♩♩♩ = ♩ ♩

A complete ratio chart looks like this:

Turn to frame 67.

Use the Shield.

Is the following example mathematically correct? $\mathbf{o} = \d\d = \eighth\eighth\eighth\eighth$

No: either the last four notes should be quarter notes (♩♩♩♩) or there should be eight eighths (♪♪♪♪♪♪♪♪).

Is this example correct?   ♪♪♪♪ = ♩♩ = ♩

yes

How about this one? Is it correct?   ♩♩♩ = ♪♪♪♪♪♪

yes

Here is one final example. Is it correct?   ♪♪♪♪♪♪♪ = ♩♩♩♩ = ♩

No: either there should be two half notes at the end (♩ ♩) or one whole note (o).

Put the Shield Aside.

By now, you may have seen that eighth notes can be written in two ways. A long series of eighth notes (♪♪♪♪♪♪♪) may be joined together and broken into groups (♫♫) to make it easier to recognize the number of notes in the series.

Now go to frame 64 and answer the Diagnostic Question.

68

Not quite. Let me explain it briefly. The pattern you chose looks like this:

$$\text{𝅗𝅥} = \text{𝅘𝅥 𝅘𝅥} = \text{𝅘𝅥𝅮𝅘𝅥𝅮} \text{ or } \text{𝅘𝅥𝅮 𝅘𝅥𝅮}$$

The first two units are correct: 𝅗𝅥 = 𝅘𝅥 𝅘𝅥. The last two units or 𝅘𝅥𝅮𝅘𝅥𝅮 , are incorrect. They are eighth notes, and it takes four eighth notes to equal two quarter notes. The correct pattern looks like this:

$$\text{𝅗𝅥} = \text{𝅘𝅥 𝅘𝅥} = \text{𝅘𝅥𝅮 𝅘𝅥𝅮 𝅘𝅥𝅮 𝅘𝅥𝅮} \text{ or } \text{𝅘𝅥𝅮𝅘𝅥𝅮𝅘𝅥𝅮𝅘𝅥𝅮}$$

If you need to review this concept further, turn to frame 66.

If not, try the last question again by returning to frame 63.

69

No, something was wrong with that alternative. Please turn to frame 66.

70

Not quite. The pattern you chose looks like this:

$$\text{𝅗𝅥} = \text{♩♩} = \text{♪♪♪♪} \text{ or } \text{♫♫ ♫♫}$$

The first three parts of the example are correct:

$$\text{𝅗𝅥} = \text{♩♩} = \text{♪♪♪♪}$$

The last group of notes ♫♫ ♫♫ is incorrect.

These are eighth notes, just like the four notes in the third group. The flags have merely been written in a different way, that is, with a beam. In other words, ♪♪ and ♫ represent the same time value.

To be correct the pattern should look like this:

$$\text{𝅗𝅥} = \text{♩♩} = \text{♪♪♪♪} \text{ or } \text{♫♫}$$

If you would like to review this concept further, turn to frame 66.

If not, try that last question again by returning to frame 63.

71

Whoops, there was an error in that response. For a better understanding of the four terms, turn to frame 65.

Diagnostic Question Four

All that is new here is the dot after the note: ♩. . Don't be misled by the fact that a dotted quarter note is used as an example; you can put dots after all other notes as well.

The dot increases a note's time value, or duration, by one-half of that note's value. The dotted note is of great importance in music because, proportionately, it is equal in value to two other notes. Can you identify the two notes that are the equivalent of a dotted quarter note?

Without guessing, choose the correct alternative below.

Alternatives

		frame
a.	I'm not sure of the answer, but I am willing to learn.	73
b.	♩. = ♩ + ♪	77
c.	♩. = 𝅗𝅥 + ♩	61
d.	♩. = ♪. + ♪	62

73

The concept of a dotted note is not difficult to comprehend. A dot is used to increase a note's time value. In fact, *a dot always increases a note's time value by one-half of that note's value.*

For example:

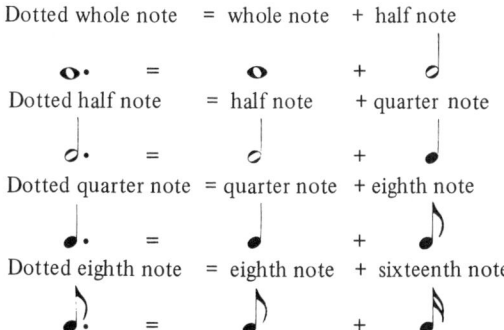

Use the Shield.

Which of the following notes has the longest time value: 𝅘𝅥· or 𝅗𝅥 ?

𝅗𝅥 ; a half note (𝅗𝅥) equals two quarter notes (𝅘𝅥 𝅘𝅥), whereas a dotted quarter note (𝅘𝅥·) equals a quarter plus an eighth (𝅘𝅥 + 𝅘𝅥𝅮).

A dotted eighth note (𝅘𝅥𝅮) has the same time value as what two notes?

𝅘𝅥𝅮· = 𝅘𝅥𝅮 + 𝅘𝅥𝅯

Go to frame 75.

74

Correct. Let's try another, similar question to make sure you understand these relationships. Go to frame 63.

75

Use the Shield.

Which two notes equal a dotted half note (𝅗𝅥.)?

𝄞

𝅗𝅥. = 𝅗𝅥 + 𝅘𝅥

Is the following example correct?

𝄞

yes

Is this example correct?

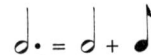

𝄞

no: 𝅗𝅥. = 𝅗𝅥 + 𝅘𝅥

Now, return to frame 72.

76

Very good, that was the right answer. You are ready for the next concept—the dotted note. Go to frame 72.

77

Good. The dot after a note increases its time value by one-half.

Hence, a dotted quarter note (♩.) is equal in value to a quarter note plus an eighth note (♩ + ♪). The dot is a handy device, but sometimes it is necessary to write in the note it represents. In music, the equivalent of the mathematical plus sign is the *tie*. For more on this subject, proceed with the next Diagnostic Question.

Diagnostic Question Five

In music notation when you want to use two notes to equal a dotted note, you *tie* the notes. "Tied" notes are connected with a curved line: ♩♪ . Remembering that a dot after a note increases its duration (time value) by one-half, choose the combination of tied notes below that are the equivalent of a dotted quarter note.

This dotted quarter note (♩.) equals:

Alternatives

		frame
a.	The two examples below look about the same to me. Please explain the difference.	80
b.	[music notation]	79
c.	[music notation]	81

78

You apparently need to review this question. The review is found in frame 85.

79

You have made a slight mistake. Please read frame 80.

80

Here is your explanation. There were two different curved-line symbols in the example.

slurred notes   tied notes

In the example on the left, the slur extending between notes on two *different* lines does not combine time values; it will be discussed later in the program. Only when the two notes are on the *same* line or space are they tied. In the example on the right, the notes are joined by a tie and have a time value equal to a dotted quarter note ( ). In the first example, the notes are not on the same line or space. Therefore, they are not tied notes.

These measures   These measures
are equal.   are equal.

Write the two tied notes that are equivalent to each of the notes given below.

ANSWERS:
(A) The half note equals two tied quarter notes.
(B) The dotted eighth equals tied eighth and sixteenth notes.
(C) The dotted half equals tied half and quarter notes.
(D) The quarter note equals tied eighth notes.

Now return to frame 77 and see if you can answer the Diagnostic Question correctly.

Correct! I'm glad you noticed that tied notes *must always be on the same line or space.*

Otherwise they are not tied notes. These notes  are connected by a tie, but the curved line between these notes  is called a *slur* and is entirely different. (The slur will be explained later in the program.) The second note of two tied notes is never sounded separately. The first note is played and held for the duration of both notes without any break. As its name implies, the tie joins them together.

The next step of the program involves *meter signatures.* For that concept continue with the next Diagnostic Question.

Diagnostic Question Six

Select the correct meaning for each number in the $\frac{3}{4}$ meter signature from the alternatives below.

Alternatives

		frame
a.	I really don't know. Please tell me.	85
b.	The 3 determines how many beats are in a measure. The 4 determines what kind of note represents the beat.	82
c.	The 3 determines what kind of note represents the beat. The 4 determines how many beats are in a measure.	78

*These are frequently called time signatures, but it is more correct to refer to them as meter signatures.

82

That's absolutely right. The top number in a meter signature determines *how many* beats will be in each measure, and the bottom number determines *what kind* of note will represent each beat. If the meter signature is $\frac{3}{4}$, there will be three beats in each measure, and each beat will be the equivalent of a quarter note.

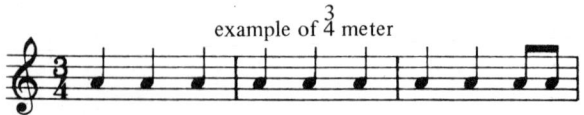

As you see in the last measure above, two eighth notes were substituted for one quarter note. This is a perfectly legitimate substitution, and such substitutions occur very frequently in music. For example:

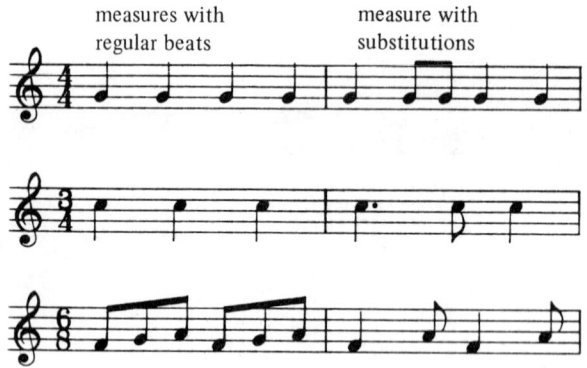

Go now to frame 84.

83

Excellent. The next question will test your understanding of meter in a slightly different way. Turn to frame 97.

Diagnostic Question Seven

Below are three musical examples with several substitutions in every measure. Can you determine the meter signature needed for each of the examples? Match the signatures listed at the right with the correct alternatives.

Signatures

1. $\frac{3}{2}$ meter

2. $\frac{2}{4}$ meter

3. $\frac{4}{4}$ meter

Alternatives

		frame
a.	I know this step of the program is very important, and I am somewhat confused. I need a more detailed discussion.	87
b.	1 = $\frac{4}{4}$ meter 2 = $\frac{3}{2}$ meter 3 = $\frac{2}{4}$ meter	96
c.	1 = $\frac{2}{4}$ meter 2 = $\frac{3}{2}$ meter 3 = $\frac{4}{4}$ meter	88
d.	1 = $\frac{3}{2}$ meter 2 = $\frac{4}{4}$ meter 3 = $\frac{2}{4}$ meter	86

The explanation is simple.

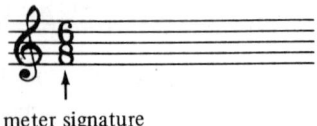

meter signature

In the above example, the meter is six-eight. A piece of music is frequently said to be in six-eight time or six-eight meter.

Six-eight meter means there is the equivalent of six eighth notes in each measure.

Three-four meter means there is the equivalent of three quarter notes in each measure.

Four-four meter means there is the equivalent of four quarter notes in each measure.

In other words, the top number of the meter signature determines *how many* beats per measure, and the bottom number determines *what kind* of note represents the beat.

6 ⟶ how many beats per measure
8 ⟶ what kind of note gets the beat

With this information, see if you can answer the question in frame 81.

You have not selected the proper alternative. To clear up the problem, carefully read the material in frame 87.

87

O.K., let's consider the matter a minute. Beside the clef sign on the staff below is a meter signature.

The bottom number of the meter signature determines *what kind* of note will be the basic beat of the measure. In three-four meter, for example, the basic beat will be the quarter note.

The top number determines *how many* of these notes will be represented in each measure. Music in $\frac{3}{4}$ meter will have the equivalent of three quarter notes in each measure. In short,

$\frac{3}{4}$ meter = 3 quarter notes (or their equivalent) per measure.

$\frac{6}{8}$ meter = 6 eighth notes (or their equivalent) per measure.

$\frac{4}{4}$ meter = 4 quarter notes (or their equivalent) per measure.

$\frac{3}{2}$ meter = 3 half notes (or their equivalent) per measure.

$\frac{9}{8}$ meter = 9 eighth notes (or their equivalent) per measure.

Please turn to frame 89.

88

You've made a mistake, but we can now try to clear the matter up. Go on to frame 87.

89

Use the Shield.

With this meter signature the basic beat of the measure will be the _____ note.

quarter (indicated by the 4)

The staff at the right is an example of _____ meter.

3/4 (3 quarter notes per measure)

This staff is an example of _____ meter.

2/4 (2 quarter notes per measure)

Here is an example of _____ meter.

6/8 (6 eighth notes per measure) or 3/4 (3 quarter notes per measure)

Put the Shield Aside.

When a meter signature designates that a measure is in three-four meter, we have the following possible simple construction:

Many variations are also possible. Here are three:

Turn to frame 90.

Each of the previous examples contained the equivalent of three quarter notes (and three beats) per measure. If each of the quarter notes were converted to eighth notes, the measure would appear:

Notice how three beats are delineated by the way the beams connecting the eighth notes are grouped.

Another meter, 6/8, may have the same number of eighth notes per measure, *but they are grouped differently.* In this example, the eighth notes are grouped into two units, or beats,

instead of three. Each beat is the equivalent of a dotted quarter note (♩.). This division into three beats rather than two beats per measure marks a fundamental difference between 3/4 meter and 6/8 meter.

Use the Shield.

Does the following measure have the correct number of beats?

no (there is an extra eighth note)

Does this measure have the correct number of beats?

yes

Which measure below is *incorrect?*

measure 3 (it needs another eighth note)

Go on to frame 91.

At first glance, you might think it difficult to determine the meter signature for the example below, but it is relatively easy.

The first two notes in the measure are eighth notes. Together they equal one quarter note. The next four notes are sixteenth notes—because of the double beam on their stems. Four sixteenth notes also equal one quarter note. Each pair of eighth notes at the end of the measure is like the one at the start. Each equals one quarter note. Thus, the measure has the equivalent of four quarter notes, as in four-four meter.

Use the Shield.

Below are a musical sample and three meter signatures. Which signature is the correct one for this music?

4/4

Which signature belongs with this sample?

3/4

Which signature is the correct one here?

4/4

Return to the Diagnostic Question in frame 84.

92

Diagnostic Question Eight

Determine the proper meter signature for each of the following examples, and select the corresponding alternative from those given below.

Alternatives

		frame
a.	If I am really honest with myself, I think a review is necessary for me to understand this question.	87
b.	$1 = \frac{4}{4};\quad 2 = \frac{3}{4};\quad 3 = \frac{4}{4}$	94
c.	$1 = \frac{3}{4};\quad 2 = \frac{6}{8};\quad 3 = \frac{4}{4}$	83
d.	$1 = \frac{3}{4};\quad 2 = \frac{2}{4};\quad 3 = \frac{6}{8}$	98

93

Sorry, that response was not accurate. You will find an explanation of this question in frame 103.

=================================== **94** ===================================

You need to take another look at the question. Read the explanation in frame 95.

=================================== **95** ===================================

The three examples were as follows:

Each measure in this example has the equal of 3 quarter notes:

meter signature: 3/4

This example has the equivalent of 6 eighth notes per measure:

meter signature: 6/8

The equivalent of 4 quarter notes per measure is in this example:

meter signature: 3/4

If you are still the least bit unsure, read the complete review in frame 87.

If not, choose the correct response for the Diagnostic Question in frame 92.

=================================== **96** ===================================

Right. You have taken a successful step toward the completion of this chapter by correctly identifying these meter signatures. Let's try another, similar problem to double-check your understanding of the important concept of meter. Go to frame 92.

══ 97 ══

Diagnostic Question Nine

The meter signature in the example below is $\frac{3}{8}$. There should be the equivalent of three eighth notes in each measure. Which measure is not correct?

Alternatives

		frame
a.	I don't know. Please explain.	103
b.	Measure 1 is incorrect.	93
c.	Measure 2 is incorrect.	110
d.	Measure 3 is incorrect.	107
e.	Measure 4 is incorrect.	102

══ 98 ══

That was not quite right. For an explanation of this question, go to frame 95.

══ 99 ══

You chose the wrong alternative, but we can clear this up very quickly. Please turn to the explanation in frame 109.

100

Not quite. Please read frame 105.

101

Diagnostic Question Ten

Each example below has one incomplete measure. In which example is the incomplete measure acceptable?

Alternatives

		frame
a.	I am not sure; I would like an explanation of this concept.	109
b.	Example 1	104
c.	Example 2	99
d.	Example 3	106

102

That alternative can't be right. When you add a quarter note and an eighth note, you have the equivalent of three eighth notes—just what the meter signature called for. For a complete explanation go to frame 103.

103

The meter was $\frac{3}{8}$. Any combination of notes equal to three eighth notes would be correct. You were to find the incorrect measure.

Measure 1 has this pattern: ♫♪ . The two sixteenth notes are equal to one eighth note. When totaled, the measure contains the equivalent of three eighth notes. It is therefore correct.

In measure 2, this pattern is found: ♩.♪ . The quarter note equals two eighth notes, and the dot after it equals another eighth note, for a total of three eighths. There is a sixteenth note left in the measure which is not needed; the measure is, therefore, incorrect.

Measure 3 has the following note pattern: ♫♫ . Each pair of sixteenth notes equals one eighth note, so the measure is complete and correct.

Measure 4 contains one quarter note and one eighth note: ♩♪ . The quarter note equals two eighth notes, when added to the existing eighth note the measure has a total of three and is correct as it stands.

Now return to frame 97.

104

You have made a mistake, so let's reconsider the question. Go to frame 109.

105

Here is an explanation.

1. Staccato: This term is applied to notes that are to be shortened slightly, so that the tones are separated from each other. Staccato is indicated by a dot above the note.

   staccato notes

2. Tenuto: This term is applied to notes that are to be held to their full duration. The mark is merely a line above the note, showing that the tone should not be cut short in any way.

   tenuto note

3. Slur: This symbol connects a series of notes. It serves basically the same purpose as the tenuto mark, but it is used when more than one tone is to be held to full length.

   slurred notes

4. Accent: An accent mark is used when one note is to be played or sung louder than the others around it.

   accented note

Now return to frame 108.

You are right! An incomplete measure is allowed at the beginning of a piece of music. The extra notes are called *pickup* notes. One well-known example is our national anthem, which begins with two pickup notes on the word "Oh."

The music begins on the third beat:

Although incomplete measures are permitted at the beginning of a piece of music, they are never permitted in the middle. In fact, to make all measures equal, the extra beat of the pickup note is usually borrowed from the last measure.

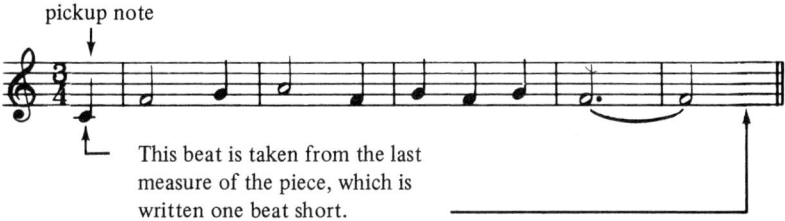

Two more examples of pickup notes follow, with numbers below the notes to show how they are counted.

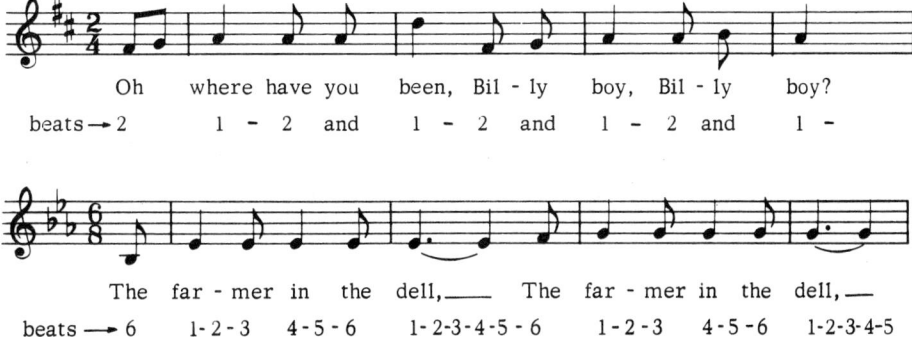

Now go to frame 108.

107

You have made a simple mistake, but not enough to be overly worried about. Let's study it for a minute in frame 103.

108

Diagnostic Question Eleven

You have now reached the last Diagnostic Question in this chapter. To answer it correctly, please read carefully.

In the three columns below, the first lists musical terms; the second shows the musical symbols used in their places; and the third column defines the symbols.

Match the three columns (your answer will be something like A-1-X or B-2-Y) and find your answer in the alternatives below.

Musical Terms	Symbols	Explanations
A. staccato	1.	W. separate the notes
B. tenuto	2.	X. hold note to full value
C. slur	3.	Y. stress this note
D. accent	4.	Z. connect the notes

Alternatives

					frame
a.	These words are strange to me. I would like an explanation.				105
b.	A-3-W,	B-2-X,	C-1-Z,	D-4-Y	111
c.	A-3-W,	B-4-Y,	C-1-X,	D-2-Z	100

You were asked if an incomplete measure is acceptable in the first measure, anywhere in the middle, or at the end of a piece.

Incomplete measures are acceptable only at the beginning of a piece of music, and at the end of a piece that begins with an incomplete measure. The notes in those incomplete measures that begin a piece are called *pickup notes.* Many well-known songs have pickup notes in them. Look at "Dixie" for example:

Another example of a pickup note is the beginning of the well-known song "Auld Lang Syne":

Now, return to the Diagnostic Question in frame 101.

Correct! You are doing very well. In fact, you don't have much further to go in this chapter. Answer the Diagnostic Question in frame 101.

That's right!

1. Staccato notes ( ) are to be separated from each other.

2. Tenuto notes ( ) are to be held to their full duration.

3. Slurred notes ( ) are to be connected. If only two notes are slurred ( ), they must be different tones or they would be *tied* notes.

4. Accented notes ( ) are to be stressed or emphasized more than the notes around them.

Congratulations, you are now at the end of Chapter 2. Please do the following exercises; they will help you use the knowledge you have just acquired.

Skill Builders

1. On the staff below, draw two notes that are tied. Then draw two notes joined by a slur.

   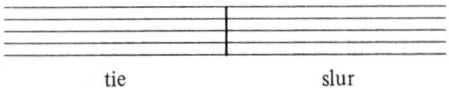

   tie   slur

2. Change the quarter notes below into eighth notes by adding flags or beams as indicated.

   flags   beams

3. Identify the meter of each of the following measures:

Please turn to frame 112.

4. Write a definition of musical rhythm in the space provided below:

5. Which musical sample below is in $\frac{6}{8}$ meter? Which is in $\frac{3}{4}$ meter?

6. Describe in writing the difference between $\frac{6}{8}$ and $\frac{3}{4}$ meter. (An explanation can be found in frame 90.)

7. The following song has no meter signature or bar lines. It should be sung in a simple flowing rhythm with pauses where the fermatas occur. Try singing it several times and notice the unique feeling of music without prescribed meter.

O COME, O COME, EMMANUEL
Thirteenth Century

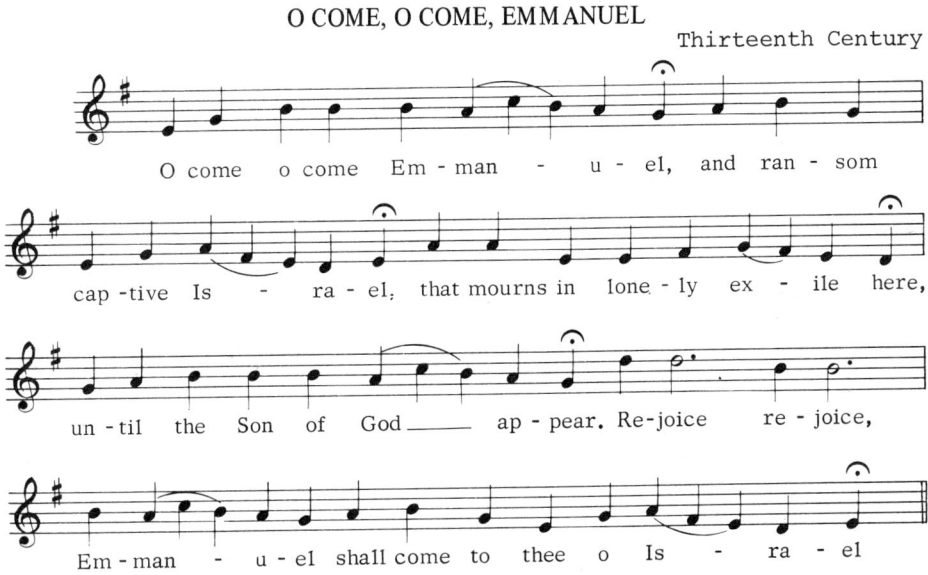

Go to frame 113.

8. Three rhythmic passages are shown below. Each passage involves different kinds of rhythmic notation. Copy each passage on the staff lines provided, making sure correct rhythms are copied, and correct rules of musical calligraphy are followed.

Turn to the next frame.

9. Now invent your own rhythmic passage and record it on the staff lines provided below. You will need to include the following steps if it is done correctly:

   (a) Determine the meter you want to employ and write that meter signature on the staff lines just after the clef sign you select.

   (b) Figure out the rhythmic passage you want to record.

   (c) Determine the correct number of notes in each desired measure of the passage.

   (d) Record each measure on the line or space of your choice.

NOTE: Do not create a rhythmic passage of complexity. You are capable of hearing and imagining passages far more difficult than you can notate. Select something simple so you can complete it successfully.

10. Now practice your rhythmic notation by copying the song "Yankee Doodle" (frame 115) on the following lines.

Continued in the next frame.

11. In the song "Yankee Doodle" locate all the dotted notes. Clap the rhythm of the song, being careful to perform the dotted notes accurately. Then sing it.

YANKEE DOODLE

1. Father and I went down to camp, a-long with Cap-tain Good-in, and there we saw the men and boys as thick as hast-y pud-din'.

Chorus: Yan-kee Doo-dle keep it up, Yan-kee Doo-dle Dan-dy, mind the mu-sic and the step and with the girls be han-dy.

Verse 2: And there we saw a thousand men, As rich as Squire David; And what they wasted every day, I wish it could be saved.

Verse 3: And there was Captain Washington, Upon a slapping stallion, A giving orders to his men; I guess there was a million.

♦ **THE NEXT STEP...**

One other concept relating to meter involves the terms *simple* and *compound*. There is disagreement among musicians as to their exact meanings, but a commonly accepted explanation follows.

Earlier in the chapter, beats (pulses) were defined as musical stresses of equal distance from each other. (In other words, stresses that are regularly spaced.)

♦   Beats: 1   2   1   2   1   2

Turn to the next frame.

♦ A universal experience in music is that such beats can be subdivided, or broken into smaller units, in at least two ways: (a) broken into units of 2, and (b) broken into units of 3.

    Beats subdivided by 2: 1 & 2 & 3 & 4 &
    Beats subdivided by 3: 1 & a 2 & a 3 & a 4 & a

RULE: If beats are subdivided by 2, the meter is referred to as *simple*.

If the beats are subdivided by 3, the meter is referred to as *compound*.

This means, for example, that the following meters are simple:

Notice that the eighth notes in the previous example are beamed into beats, and that all beat units are duple. According to the same rule, the following meters are compound because each beamed unit (beat) is subdivided by 3.

A very common question is hereby answered, namely; "What is the difference between $\frac{3}{4}$ and $\frac{6}{8}$ meters?" The answer is that $\frac{3}{4}$ meter is simple, and $\frac{6}{8}$ meter is compound.

Having now explored the nature of simple and compound meters, can you find some songs that are in compound meters? As you find them, be sure to experience the quality of the triple subdivisions of the beats. It is clearly a different quality from ♦ that of simple meters.

Turn to frame 117.

Self - Test

1. "Farmer in the Dell" has been printed below without bar lines, except for the first measure. Fill in the remaining bar lines for the complete song.

FARMER IN THE DELL

Verse 2: The farmer takes a wife.
Verse 3: The wife takes a child.
Verse 4: The child takes a dog.
Verse 5: The dog takes a cat.
Verse 6: The cat takes a mouse.
Verse 7: The mouse takes some cheese.
Verse 8: The cheese stands alone.

Please turn to frame 118.

2. "Little Tom Tinker" has been printed below without bar lines, except for the first measure. Write in the remaining bar lines for the complete song.

LITTLE TOM TINKER

3. On what words in "Farmer in the Dell" or "Little Tom Tinker" is a *slur* employed?

4. On what words in either song is a *tie* employed?

5. What beat does the pickup note get in "Farmer in the Dell"?

6. Which measure below has the *incorrect* number of beats in it?

Please turn to frame 119.

On the left are a series of dotted notes and tied notes. On the right, mathematical equivalents of each example are listed randomly. Select a letter for each number and write it in the proper blank.

Choose the proper meter signature for each of the six music samples below and record your answer in the proper blank.

Please turn to frame 120.

Match the expression marks on the left with the proper definition from the right.

21. ____ 𝅘𝅥̄   A. Staccato note: to be separated from other notes.

22. ____ 𝅗𝅥 (>)   B. Tied quarter notes: equal to one half note.

23. ____ 𝅘𝅥.   C. Tenuto note: to be held to its full duration.

24. ____ 𝅘𝅥‿𝅘𝅥   D. Accented note: to be given more stress than the surrounding notes.

Match each of the terms on the left with the appropriate definition from those provided on the right.

25. ____ rhythm   A. the rate of movement in music

                                        B. to play tones in a detached manner

26. ____ pulse   C. regularly spaced beats in music

27. ____ meter   D. a word that designates the loudness or softness in music

28. ____ tempo   E. the organization of beats into identifiable groups

                                        F. the progression of musical sounds through time

You Have Now Competed the Self-Test.

Check your answers with the key that follows and grade your results. If you missed a substantial number of the items, you should read the chapter again before going on. In any case, be sure to review each question you missed before proceeding. (The signal ff indicates the review continues to other parts.)

Turn to frame 121.

Answers & Review Index

1. "Farmer in the Dell." Put bar lines in the following places: line one: before the word *dell*, before *far-mer*, before *dell*, after *dell*. (meter signatures, 87 ff)
line two: before *der-ry*, before *far-mer*, before *dell*.

2. "Little Tom Tinker." Put bar lines in the following places: line one: before the word *he*, after *to*; line two: after the rest following *cry*. (meter signatures, 87ff) before the second *ma*, before *poor*, before *guy*.

3. In "Little Tom Tinker," line two, the words *ma, ma*. (slur and tie, 80)

4. In "Farmer in the Dell," the word *dell* employs a tie three times.
In "Little Tom Tinker," on the words *cry* and *guy*. (slur and tie, 80)

5. The sixth (last) count of the measure. (pickup notes, 109)

6. Measure 3 (meter signatures, 87 ff)

7. C (tied notes, 80)

8. H (dotted notes, 73)

9. F (tied notes, 80)

10. A (tied notes, 80)

11. G (dotted notes, 73)

12. B (dotted notes, 73)

13. D (dotted notes, 73)

14. E (tied notes, 80)

15. $\frac{2}{4}$ meter (meter signatures, 87 ff)

16. $\frac{3}{4}$ meter (meter signatures, 87 ff)

17. $\frac{6}{8}$ meter (meter signatures, 87 ff)

18. $\frac{6}{4}$ meter (meter signatures, 87 ff)

19. $\frac{4}{4}$ meter (meter signatures, 87 ff)

Please continue on the following page.

20. $\frac{3}{8}$ meter (meter signatures, 87)
21. C (tenuto mark, 105)
22. D (accented note, 105)
23. A (staccato note, 105)
24. B (tied notes, 80)
25. F (definition, 65)
26. C (definition, 65)
27. E (definition, 65)
28. A (definition, 65)

Now review all the items missed. Then proceed with Chapter 3.

3
Basic Components of Pitch

123

Music as we know it seldom consists of rhythm alone. It also includes pitch, the subject of this chapter. You will recall from Chapter 1 how to locate the highest and lowest notes in a passage of music. Now it is time to consider all the notes on a staff, how the staff is used as a framework for notating pitch, and how the staff is related to a piano keyboard. A system of organizing notes, or tones, into scales based on a particular key tone will also be introduced.

Objectives

At the conclusion of this chapter, you will be asked to demonstrate your knowledge of the music staff by:

1. Recognizing a definition of pitch.
2. Recalling the names of notes on the treble staff.
3. Recalling the names of notes on the bass staff.
4. Matching the symbols for sharps, flats, and naturals with their proper descriptions.
5. Identifying an octave on the staff.
6. Recognizing the function of ledger lines.

Using a replica of the piano keyboard, you will be asked to do the following:

1. Recall from memory the names of the notes of the white keys.
2. Demonstrate an understanding of the relationship between sharps and flats and the black keys.
3. Identify an octave on the piano keyboard.
4. Identify whole steps and half steps.

In this chapter there will be twelve Diagnostic Questions. Now turn to frame 124.

124

Diagnostic Question One*

The highness or lowness of a tone is called its *pitch*. As you learned earlier, the pitch of a note is reflected by its placement on the staff. The higher it is placed on the staff, the higher its pitch; the lower it is on the staff, the lower its pitch.

Notes can be placed on any line or any space of the staff, depending on the pitch desired. Each of these lines and spaces has a letter name—A, B, C, D, E, F, or G. After the G, the pitches start over again with A. There is no such note as H.

Can you identify the notes of the treble clef on the staff below? If so, choose the alternative that properly identifies all the notes from left to right. Then turn to the frame indicated.

Alternatives

		frame
a.	I'm not familiar with this aspect of music. Please explain it.	126
b.	C G A E D	132
c.	B G F E D	139
d.	B F G D C	133

125

You are right. For your next question go to frame 143.

*If you have already answered the question once, correctly answer it again and continue the program as directed.

The names of the notes on the treble staff are easy to learn once you understand the system for naming lines and spaces of the staff. We'll start with the note *middle C*—found on a ledger line between the treble and the bass clef.

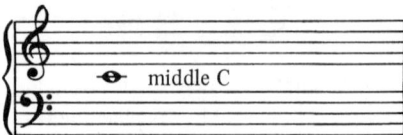

The middle C line serves the same purpose as the other lines of the staff. The space above it is D, and the notes continue to rise on the staff in alphabetical order: C, D, E, F, G. After G, the musical alphabet starts over again with A (see example below).

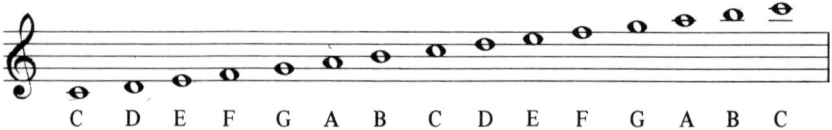

Notice that every line and every space is given a note, including the notes above the staff, which fall on ledger lines.

Use the Shield.

This note, because it is between the treble and bass clefs, is called middle _____.

🙢

C

The note directly above middle C is _____.

🙢

D

The fourth note above middle C is called _____.

🙢

G

Go to frame 127.

127

Use the Shield.

After G, the letters start over again with _____.

A

An easy way to remember the names of the spaces is to notice the word they spell when read from bottom to top.

From bottom to top, the spaces spell the word _____.

FACE

Once you know the names of the spaces you can figure out the names of the other notes.
From left to right, these notes are _____, _____, and _____.

F, A, and G

When notes are written above or below the regular staff *ledger lines* are used. Nonetheless, every line and space is utilized. The names of these notes are , _____, _____, and _____.

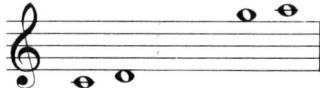

Turn to frame 129 for the answer.

128

You are apparently confused about the notes. A review is found in frame 131.

129

C, D, G, A

Use the Shield.

These notes are _____,
_____, and _____.

E, D, F (E is the top space and, therefore, the last letter in the word FACE.)

What word do these notes spell?

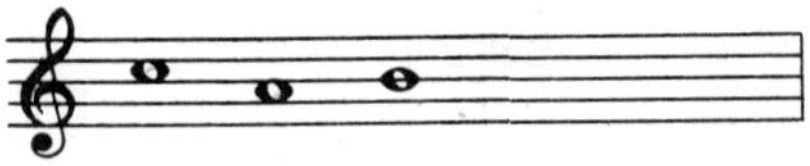

CAB

What word do these notes spell?

AGE

Do these two notes have the same name? What are their names?

Yes: They are both C, and the lower one (on a ledger line) is called middle C.

These notes tell you what many people like to do. They like to _____.

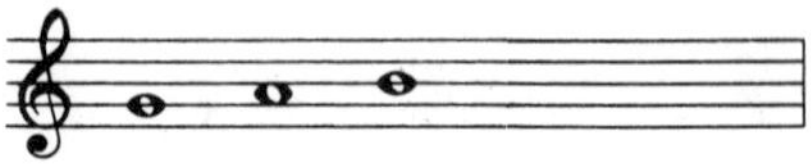

GAB

Turn to frame 147.

130

You seem to have confused the notes. You will find the explanation you need in frame 138.

Sorry, this explanation will help you avoid another mistake.

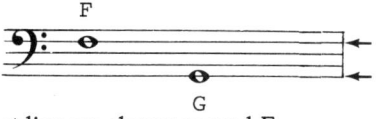

The two notes on the staff at the right are important ones for you to memorize immediately. Notice the two dots in the bass clef sign and the line between. Notes on that line are always named F.

The other important note—on the bottom line of the staff—is always called G. By remembering the names of these two notes, you can determine the other notes in the bass clef. For example, a note on the space right above G would be A. (Remember, notes go from A to G and then start over with A.)

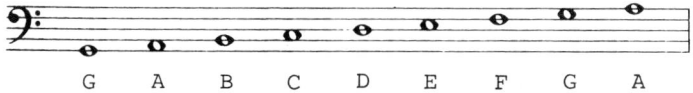

Be sure to assign a note to every line and every space. By being careful not to skip a line or a space, and by remembering the two key notes in the example at the top of the page, you will find it easy to recall the notes of the bass clef.

If you would like to do a short exercise on the bass clef, turn to frame 140. If not, return to the question in frame 143.

The alternative you selected was not quite right. Take a close look at the notes on the staff below. The note on the first line below the staff is middle C.

C D E F G A B C

After middle C, the notes go up alphabetically, falling alternately on each line and each space, to G. Then, they start over again with A and continue as before. Here is a speedy way to remember the notes of the treble clef:

1. Learn middle C and the space above it (D).

2. Learn the names of the spaces, from the bottom to the top. (They spell the word FACE.)

3. If you need to identify a line, determine what the space directly below it is named, and then go up alphabetically.

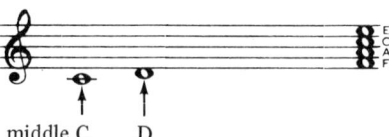

middle C   D

If a drill on the notes of the treble clef will help fix them in your mind, go to frame 126. If you are sure that you know the notes, return to frame 124.

Right. Let's see if you can do as well with the musical example in the following Diagnostic Question.

Diagnostic Question Two

What are the names of the notes on this staff?

Alternatives

		frame
a.	I need to review this concept.	126
b.	E F A G F E D	134
c.	B F A G F E C	141
d.	B F E D C A G	146

You seem to be confused and in need of an explanation on the notes of the treble clef. Go on to frame 135.

The note on the first line below the staff is middle C.

After middle C, the notes go up the staff alphabetically, falling alternately on lines and spaces. After G (the second line of the treble clef), the notes start over alphabetically with A and continue as before, even when they go above the staff, and ledger lines are used.

A speedy way to remember the notes of the treble clef is to use the following steps:

1. Learn middle C and the note (D) in the space directly above it.

2. Learn the names of the spaces, from the bottom to the top. They spell the word FACE.

3. When you need to identify a line, first determine the letter name of the space directly under it and then go up alphabetically.

middle C

If you would like a detailed exercise now, turn to frame 126. If you don't think you need the exercise, return to frame 133 and answer the Diagnostic Question.

136

Diagnostic Question Three*

The lines and spaces of the bass clef do not have the same names as those in the treble clef. In the example below are several notes in the bass clef. Can you identify the notes and select the corresponding alternative from those listed?

Alternatives

		frame
a.	I don't know the notes of the bass clef. Where is an explanation?	138
b.	G B C D E G	150
c.	G D E F G B	125
d.	A C D E F B	130

*If you have already answered the question once, correctly answer it again and continue the program as directed.

137

You were mistaken in your choice. A good review is available in frame 144. Please turn there now.

138

Notes in the bass clef are alphabetical, just as in the treble clef. They also go from A through G and then begin over with A. However, they must be learned separately because they fall on different lines and spaces of the staff.

The first two notes you need to learn are F and G.

In the example, observe the bass clef sign with its two dots, and the staff line between the dots. *The line between the dots of the bass clef sign is always called F.* Thus, the note you see on that line is F.

The second note you need to remember is on the bottom line of the staff—the G line. Memorize these two notes, and from them you can figure out all other notes in the bass clef. For example, a note on the bottom space (right above G) would be A. (Remember, notes go from A to G and then start over with A.) All the notes in the bass clef are shown below.

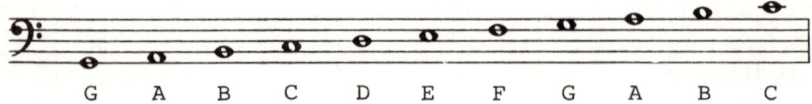

Turn to frame 140.

139

No, you started out right on B, but the other notes were incorrect. For an explanation, go to frame 126.

140

Use the Shield.

Probably the easiest note to learn in the bass clef is found on the line between the dots of the bass clef sign. That note is _____.

🔔

F

Another important note in the bass clef is found on the bottom line. That note is _____.

🔔

G

Counting one note for each line and one note for each space above G, this note is found to be _____.

🔔

C

In both the treble and bass clefs, notes are named A, B, C, D, E, F, G. The note after G is always _____.

🔔

A

This note is on the space directly under F. It is named _____.

🔔

E

From left to right, these notes spell a word. What is the word?

🔔

FAD

Turn to frame 142.

141

Right. You have again identified the notes in the treble clef correctly, including one on a ledger line above the treble staff. Now go to frame 136.

142

Use the Shield.

From left to right, what word do these notes spell?

👉

AGE

Do these three notes spell a word?

👉

Yes, BEG

These notes do not spell a word. What are their names?

👉

A, F, G, and C

What long word do these notes spell?

👉

BAGGAGE

If you feel the need for more review, reread the material that begins in frame 138. If not, return to frame 136.

143

Diagnostic Question Four

Now try this longer series of notes in the bass clef. Name the notes in the following example:

Alternatives

		frame
a.	I could use a review.	138
b.	G E B C A G C	148
c.	G E B C A F C	131
d.	G E C B A G C	128

144

While learning the names of notes from A to G, you also learned the position of middle C on the staff—between the bass and treble clefs.

The first note to learn on the piano is also middle C. You might wonder how many notes are named C on the keyboard. There are quite a few—one for every octave.

In the picture of the keyboard below, notice that the black keys are arranged in groups of two or three. These groups are repeated up and down the keyboard.

The first thing you need to remember is that the notes A, B, C, D, E, F, G are the long, white keys. The black keys are for sharps or flats.

Directly to the *left* of the two black keys is C. Find C on the picture of the keyboard. Between the two black keys and right next to C, is D. Then come E, F, G, A, and B (all white keys). Then the notes start over with C again.

For the present you should fix in your mind two particular white keys: the C directly left of the two black keys, and the F directly left of the three black keys. Find F on the keyboard.

Turn to frame 152.

145

That alternative was incorrect. See if this review will freshen your memory.

There are two keys you need to recognize quickly when you look at a keyboard. The first is directly left of the two black keys (number 1). It is C. The second key is F, which is directly left of the three black keys (number 2).

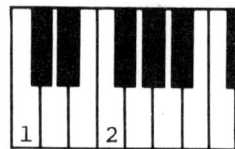

Remember also that the notes A, B, C, D, E, F, and G are the white keys. The black keys are used for sharps and flats.

By remembering the places of C and F on the keyboard, you can determine all the other notes. *Study the above example before going on.*

The above discussion is intended only as a short reminder. If you have not had previous experience with the piano keyboard, or if you feel that you need a longer review, turn to frame 144.

If you are sure the above discussion is a sufficient reminder, return to the Diagnostic Question in frame 157.

146

You made a mistake and need an explanation to clarify the problem. Go to frame 135.

147

Use the Shield.

These notes spell _____.

❧

BADGE

Here is a longer one.
The word is _____.

❧

CABBAGE

These notes spell _____.

❧

DEED

These letters do not spell a word.
The notes are ____, ____, ____,
____, ____.

❧

F, B, A, D, B

Now return to frame 124 and see if you can answer the Diagnostic Question.

148

Good. Until now we have been dealing with music as it is written on the staff. Obviously, music must be played or sung to be heard. The most common musical instrument is the human voice, but many other instruments (piano, organ, and harpsichord) employ a keyboard. It is now time to become acquainted with the keyboard.

Go to frame 149.

Diagnostic Question Five*

A section of the piano keyboard is pictured below. Notice that the short black keys are in alternating groups of two and three.

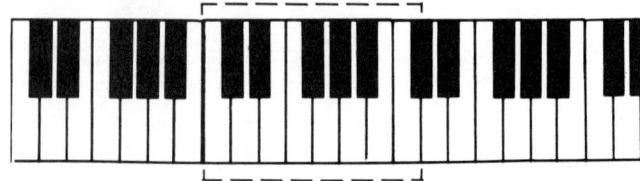

When a picture of the keyboard is used hereafter, only a small section—like the one within the dotted lines—will be shown.

Every key on the piano will sound a note, and that note can be written on the staff. The notes on the piano keyboard have the same names as notes on the staff (A, B, C, D, E, F, G, A, B, etc.), and you should learn them.

In the section of the keyboard pictured below, five keys are numbered. Can you select the correct alternative by identifying the letter name of each numbered key?

Alternatives

						frame
a.	I am not familiar with the piano keyboard. Will you explain it to me?					144
b.	1 = B,	2 = A,	3 = D,	4 = C,	5 = F	137
c.	1 = E,	2 = F,	3 = G,	4 = A,	5 = D	154
d.	1 = E,	2 = G,	3 = D,	4 = F,	5 = B	156

*If you have already answered this question once, correctly answer it again and continue the program.

150

Some of the notes in this answer are right, but you did make a mistake.

Two lines are particularly important for remembering notes in the bass clef. Do you see the two dots in the bass clef sign? Between them is the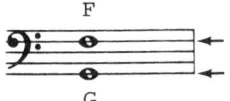
first important line. Notes on that line are always named F. The bottom line of the bass staff is always called G. From those two notes you can determine the other notes on the clef. For example, a note on the first space (right above G) would be A. As in the treble clef, the notes go from A to G and then start over with A.

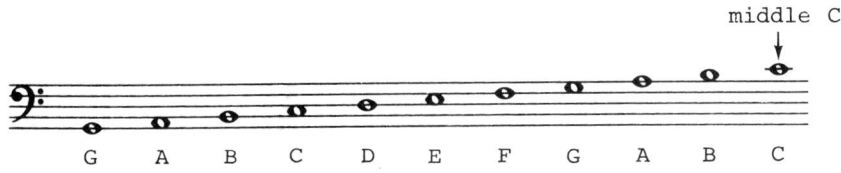

Be sure to assign a letter to every line and every space. By being careful not to skip notes, and by remembering the two key lines illustrated in the example at the top of the page, you can readily recall the notes of the bass clef.

If you would like to do a short exercise on the bass clef, turn to frame 140. If you feel that the exercise is not necessary, return to frame 136.

151

You missed one note and should review the subject. There's a brief review for you in frame 145.

152

Use the Shield.

On the piano keyboard the sharps and flats are generally found on the _____ keys.

◆§

black

The notes A, B, C, D, E, F, and G are on the _____ keys.

◆§

white

The black keys are in groups of two and three. Directly left of the two black keys is the note _____.

◆§

C

The arrow in this example is pointing to the note _____.

◆§

C

Does C appear on the keyboard more than one time?

◆§

yes

The white key directly right of C is _____.

◆§

D

The key to the left of the three black notes is the note _____.

◆§

F

Turn to frame 153.

Use the Shield.

In this picture, number 1 is the note
_____, and number 2 is the note
_____.

◆

C, F

Here, number 1 is the note _____,
and number 2 is the note _____.

◆

D, G

What are the names of notes 1, 2, and
3 here?

◆

E, F, A

What are the names of the numbered
notes here?

◆

D, E, A

Of the numbered notes, which
is A?

◆

2

Which key in that last frame is E?

◆

1

What key is number 3 in the example above?

◆

B

Now return to the Diagnostic Question in frame 149.

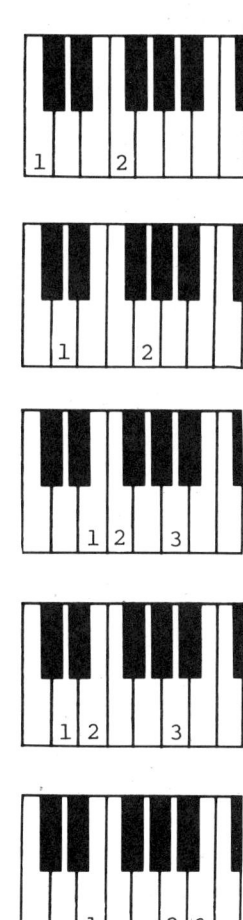

154

No, that wasn't entirely correct. For an explanation of this question, go to frame 144.

155

No, you are mistaken, but the mistake is easy to correct.

If you start at the left of the keyboard and play every note (that is, every white and black key) from left to right, you are playing *half steps*. A half step is the smallest step on the piano keyboard. *Every note is one half step from its closest neighbor.*

Even if two white keys do not have a black key between them, the two keys are still a half step apart. (See the example.)

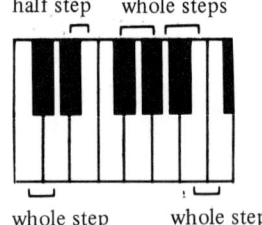

Notice, however, that if there is a key between the two given keys, they are a whole step apart.

Return to the Diagnostic Question in frame 181.

Excellent. Here's hoping you can do as well on the next question, which is similar. Go to frame 157.

Diagnostic Question Six

Choose the alternative which properly identifies all five keys numbered below.

Alternatives

				frame
a.	I am uncertain about this question.			144
b.	1 = G 2 = C	3 = E 4 = B 5 = C		160
c.	1 = D 2 = F	3 = B 4 = E 5 = G		145
d.	1 = G 2 = F	3 = E 4 = B 5 = C		151

158

Here is an explanation of half steps. The smallest unit that can be notated in traditional musical notation is a half step.

On standard keyboard instruments, a half step is the distance from any key to its nearest neighbor. Look, for example, at the note D on the keyboard to the right. Is E the closest note to D? The answer is "no" because there is a black key between them. That black key is named either D-sharp or E-flat. (Both names are correct.) From D to D-sharp is a half step, but from D to E is 2 half steps or 1 whole step.

Now turn to frame 162.

159

The black keys are causing you some confusion. Read carefully the explanation in frame 170.

160

You chose the proper alternative, and are ready to do something else. Go to frame 161.

161

Diagnostic Question Seven

The purpose of this question is to check your understanding of the nature of half steps, sharps, flats, and naturals. If you do not understand these concepts, choose alternative one. Otherwise, answer the question correctly.

Question: Which of the following intervals is a half step?

Alternatives

		frame
a.	I am not sure.	158
b.	C to D	163
c.	D to E	165
d.	E to F	166

162

A half step, then, is the interval between any note and its nearest neighbor. What kind of symbol is used to indicate half steps? Well, you have a choice. You can use a sharp with the bottom note, D. *The sharp raises the pitch of a note by one half step.* The new note, called D-sharp, would be halfway between D and E.

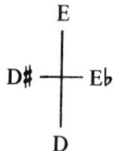

The other alternative is to use a flat with the top note, E. *A flat lowers the pitch of the note by one half step.* The new note is called E-flat. The two notes appear to be different on the staff, but their sound is the same. They are enharmonic spellings of the same pitch.

A related musical symbol is the natural: ♮ . *A natural cancels the effect of previous sharps or flats.* For example, if you wanted to write three notes in a row; C, then C-sharp, and C again, you would put a natural sign in front of the last C to tell the performer to cancel the effect of the previous sharp. (See the example below.)

The first note and the third note are the same. The natural sign would not be necessary if the middle note were removed.

Turn to frame 164.

163

I'm sorry, that was not the correct answer. Please turn to frame 158.

164

Use the Shield.

From B to C is a half step.
(Yes or no)

Yes. There is no black key between them.

From F to G is a (*whole/half*) step.

Whole step. There is a black key between them.

What note is one half step above C?

C-sharp (the black key)

Which of the following intervals is a half step?
A to B, or B to C, or C to D

B to C is the only half step among the three.

What is the interval from F-sharp to G-sharp?

A whole step. There is a white key between them.

Now return to frame 161 and answer the question.

165

I'm sorry, that was not the correct answer. An explanation is found in frame 158.

166

You are right. A half step is the distance from any key on a keyboard to its nearest neighbor. From the note E the nearest note above is F, which is a half step higher. The nearest note below E is E-flat (or D-sharp), which is a half step lower. Now read the next Diagnostic Question just below.

Diagnostic Question Eight

Not only do the white keys of the piano have names, but the black keys have names as well. Identify the numbered black keys in the following example to pick your alternative.

Alternatives

		frame
a.	I think I should let you show me.	167
b.	1 = G♭ or F♯ 3 = A♭ or G♯ 2 = D♭ or C♯ 4 = B♯ or C♭ 5 = C♯ or D♭	159
c.	1 = F♯ or G♭ 3 = A♭ or G♯ 2 = D♯ or E♭ 4 = A♯ or B♭ 5 = D♭ or C♯	169
d.	1 = F♯ or G♭ 3 = A♯ or B♭ 2 = E♭ or D♯ 4 = B♯ or C♭ 5 = C♯ or D♭	170

The first thing to remember about black keys is that they are used only as sharps and flats. You also need to understand that a black key can have two names.

The black key in the example on the right is between F and G. It can be called F-sharp because it is directly above F; or it can be called G-flat because it is directly below G. Both names are correct; they refer to the same note. Let's look at another example:

Black key number 1 is halfway between D and E. Therefore, the key can be called D-sharp or E-flat. Either name is correct, depending on the music in which the note is used.

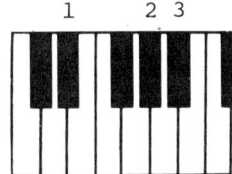

Black key number 2 is between G and A. It can, therefore, be called G-sharp or A-flat. Black key 3, between A and B, can be called A-sharp or B-flat. Thus, every black key has two possible names.

Use the Shield.

This black key between C and D can be called C-sharp or _____.
Either name is correct.

◈

D-flat

This black key between F and G, therefore, can be called either _____ sharp or _____ flat.

◈

F-sharp, G-flat

The two names of this black key are _____ and _____.

◈

A-sharp, B-flat

Continue in frame 168.

168

Use the Shield.

Which black key is D-flat?

🙶
number 1

Another name for the key we call D-flat is _____.

🙶
C-sharp

The two names for the key under number 3 are _____ and _____.

🙶
F-sharp, G-flat

A-sharp (B-flat) is found under number _____.

🙶
5

Number 4 is G-sharp or _____.

🙶
A-flat

Now carefully choose the correct answer to the Diagnostic Question in frame 166.

169

That was a good choice. Obviously, you realize that a black key between two white keys has two names.

The black key between C and D can properly be called either C-sharp (because it is directly above C) or D-flat (because it is directly below D).

Now we must return to the word "octave," which you learned earlier.

The next step in the program is in frame 172.

Some of the notes you identified were incorrect.

Here are four points for you to remember:

1. The black keys are used for sharps and flats only.
2. Every black key has two names, one using a sharp (♯), and the other using a flat (♭).
3. Every black key is between two white keys. For example, this one is between C and and D:

4. The black key is named by putting a sharp with the name of the lower white key (here, C-sharp), or by putting a flat with the name of the higher white key (here, D-flat). Both C-sharp and D-flat are correct names for this black key.

The same is true with any black key. *If you find the names of the two white keys on either side,* and *put a sharp with the lower one, or a flat with the higher one*, you will have the black-key name.

This was only a short review. If the concept of black keys still seems at all strange to you, turn to frame 167.

If this review is sufficient, return to the Diagnostic Question in frame 166 and see if you can answer it correctly.

No, that is too small for an octave. To learn why, turn to frame 176.

172

Diagnostic Question Nine

Another term you should know is *octave*. Which of the measures below (1, 2, or 3) is an example of an octave?

Alternatives

		frame
a.	I don't know, please explain.	175
b.	measure 1	177
c.	measure 2	178
d.	measure 3	180

173

Well, you've made an error. You should read the explanation on keyboard octaves. Go to frame 176.

174

That is correct. An octave is the distance from A to A, B to B, C to C, and so forth, whether on the staff or on the keyboard. For the next step go to frame 181.

175

You were asked to identify an octave. Recall that the notes of the staff are named from A through G, and then they start over again with A. The distance from one A through the next A is called an octave. B through B, C through C, D through D, and so forth, are also octaves.

Which measure has the octave in this example?

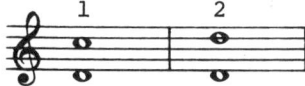

In measure 1 the bottom note is D. It is one step above middle C. Counting up one note for each line and each space, the top note in measure 1 is C. D to C is not an octave.

In measure number 2 the bottom note is still D, but the top note is one step higher than before. The top note in measure 2 is D. From D to D is an octave, so measure 2 is the correct answer.

Now return to the Diagnostic Question in frame 172.

176

When we first used the term *octave*, we were talking about the music staff. If you start with A on the staff and proceed through G, you must continue to A to complete the octave. It is exactly the same on the piano keyboard. An octave is the distance from A to A, B to B, C to C, and so forth, whether on the staff or on the keyboard.

When asked to find an octave on the keyboard, you first need to name the starting key. Then, count up the musical alphabet until you arrive at the same letter name you started with. In so doing, you will cover an octave.

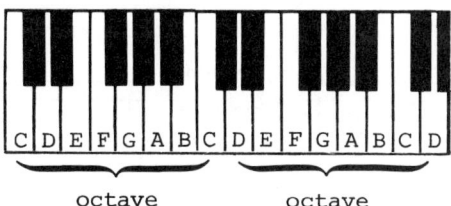

Two octaves are marked in the above example (C to C, and D to D). There are many other octaves shown as well: E to E, F to F, A to A, etc.

Briefly, to find an octave on the keyboard, identify any key and find the nearest key with the same letter name. An octave is located between these two keys.

Now you should find it easy to identify the octave in frame 177.

177

Correct. Another question about octaves follows.

Diagnostic Question Ten

At the base of the keyboard below are three numbered arrows. One of them covers exactly an octave on the keyboard; the other two do not. Which arrow points out an octave?

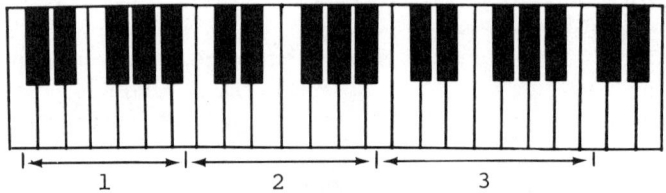

Alternatives

		frame
a.	I'm not sure which arrow points out an octave. Please explain.	176
b.	Arrow 1	171
c.	Arrow 2	174
d.	Arrow 3	173

178

No, you seem to need an explanation. Go to frame 175.

179

You've overlooked an important point. To discover it go to frame 182.

No, not quite. To understand why, go to frame 175.

Diagnostic Question Eleven

In the next example, the brackets show the two locations on the keyboard where there are no black keys between the white keys.

If there is *no* black key between two white keys, the white keys are said to be:

Alternatives

		frame
a.	one half step apart	184
b.	one whole step apart	155

182

The problem is to find the white keys on a piano keyboard that are only one half step apart. Do you recall the statement made earlier that every key is only one half step from its nearest neighboring key, black or white?

Look at the note C in the example. The nearest key to the right of C is the black key C-sharp. Therefore, the distance from C to C-sharp is one half step. From the black key C-sharp to its nearest neighbor (D) is also one half step. Thus, there are two half steps from C to D—or one whole step.

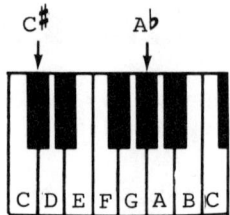

We can conclude the following: If there is one key between any two given keys, the two given keys are *one whole step* apart. If there is no key between them, the keys are one half step apart. For example, from C to D is a whole step because there is a black key between them. G to A-flat is a half step because there is no note between them.

When you are asked to show which white keys are only one half step apart, the white keys *without black keys between them* are the ones you must find. Keep that in mind as you complete the following exercises.

Continue in frame 186.

183

Your answer was partially right but you need a brief explanation. You will find it in frame 182.

184

Right. If there is no black key between two white keys, the white keys are a half step apart. If there is a black key between them, the white keys are a whole step apart. Please continue with the next Diagnostic Question below.

Diagnostic Question Twelve

Which white keys in this example are only one half step from each other?

Alternatives

		frame
a.	I believe you should explain it.	182
b.	E to F only	183
c.	E to F and B to C	187
d.	C to D and F to G	179

185

Verse 7. Can she make a cherry pie, Billy Boy, Billy Boy?
Can she make a cherry pie, charmin' Billy?
She can make a cherry pie quick as a cat can wink her eye,
She's a young thing and cannot leave her mother.

Verse 8. Does she often go to church, Billy Boy, Billy Boy?
Does she often go to church, charmin' Billy?
Yes she often goes to church, with her bonnet white as birch,
She's a young thing and cannot leave her mother.

Verse 9. Can she make a pudding well, Billy Boy, Billy Boy?
Can she make a pudding well, charmin' Billy?
She can make a pudding well, I can tell it by the smell,
She's a young thing and cannot leave her mother.

186

Use the Shield.

On the piano keyboard the distance from C to D is a _____ step.

🙾

whole *(There is a black key between them.)*

From B to C is a _____ step.

🙾

half *(No key is between.)*

From G to A-flat is a _____ step.

🙾

half

From F-sharp to G-sharp is a _____ step.

🙾

whole *(The key G is between.)*

From E to F-sharp is a _____ step.

🙾

whole *(F is between.)*

Now return to the Diagnostic Question in frame 184.

187

Congratulations. You remembered that the distance from one key to its nearest neighbor is always a half step. Therefore, the half steps are between E and F, and B and C. By learning the location of half steps, you have completed the last Diagnostic Question in the chapter. Turn now to the next frame.

And then laughed Peter merrily,	*Da lachte selbst der Petrus,*
Ho-ho, ho-ho, ho-ho,	*Ho-ho, ho-ho, ho-ho*
And then laughed Peter merrily,	*Da lachte selbst der Petrus,*
Ho-ho, ho-ho, ho-ho!	*Ho-ho, ho-ho, ho-ho!*

And so the heavens did rejoice,	*Da lacht' das ganze Himmelreich,*
Ha-ha, he-he, ho-ho,	*Ha-ha, hi-hi, ho-ho,*
And so the heavens did rejoice,	*Da lacht' das ganze Himmelreich,*
Ha-ha, he-he, ho-ho!	*Ha-ha, hi-hi, ho-ho!*

2. Find a piano, organ, set of bells, xylophone, or any other keyboard instrument and count the number of notes named "C" on it. Then do the same thing for several other notes as well. Are there the same number of notes bearing each name, or does the number vary?

3. While sitting in front of a keyboard, close your eyes and touch one of the notes. Open your eyes and identify it. Repeat the process until you can name the notes rapidly.

4. Practice saying the names of the notes in "Alouette." Then say the names of the notes in the correct rhythm. Practice playing the melody on some musical instrument.

ALOUETTE

French Canadian Folk Song

Verse 2. Je te plumerai le bec.　　*Verse 4.* Je te plumerai le dos.
Verse 3. Je te plumerai le nez.　　*Verse 5.* Je te plumerai le cou.

Please go to frame 191.

5. Practice playing the top line of "Billy Boy" with your right hand on the piano keyboard. After rehearsing your left hand alone as well, practice playing the entire piece with both hands. If no piano is available, use another instrument that has a keyboard, playing either hand, or both hands if possible.

BILLY BOY

Verse 2. Did she ask you to come in, Billy Boy, Billy Boy?
Did she ask you to come in, charmin' Billy?
She did ask me to come in, with a dimple in her chin,
She's a young thing and cannot leave her mother.

Continued on the following page.

Verse 3. Did she ask you to sit down, Billy Boy, Billy Boy?
Did she ask you to sit down, charmin' Billy?
Yes she asked me to sit down, with a curtsey to the ground,
She's a young thing and cannot leave her mother.

Verse 4. Did she set for you a chair, Billy Boy, Billy Boy?
Did she set for you a chair, charmin' Billy?
Yes she set for me a chair, she has ringlets in her hair,
She's a young thing and cannot leave her mother.

Verse 5. How old is she, Billy Boy, Billy Boy?
How old is she, charmin' Billy?
Three times six, four times seven, twenty eight and eleven,
She's a young thing and cannot leave her mother.

Verse 6. How tall is she, Billy Boy, Billy Boy?
How tall is she charmin' Billy?
She's as tall as any pine, and as straight as a pumpkin vine.
She's a young thing and cannot leave her mother.

Additional verses may be found in frame 185.

6. Copy the following clef signs and key signatures on the blank staves below:

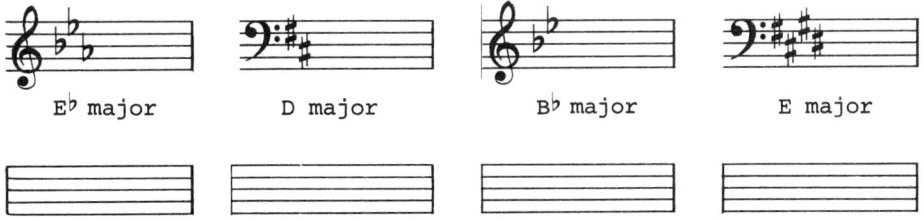

7. On the left keyboard below are brackets that show two half steps. Mark in the same way at least 10 other half steps on that keyboard. On the right keyboard are brackets identifying whole steps. Mark at least 10 whole steps on that keyboard.

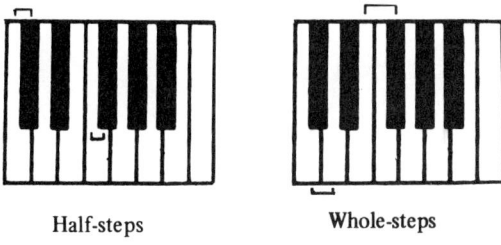

Please continue in the next frame.

8. On the staff lines below, practice writing both pitch and rhythmic notation by copying one of the songs, "There Was a Woman, Old and Gray"; "Alouette"; or "Billy Boy."

The Self-Test for Chapter 3 can be found on the next page.

Self-Test

Match the musical terms and symbols on the left side of the page with their proper definitions from the list on the right.

1. pitch _____
2. octave _____
3. half step _____
4. sharp _____
5. flat _____
6. natural _____
7. whole step _____

A. the interval from any note to its nearest neighbor
B. raises the pitch of a note by one half step
C. the distance from A to B or C to D
D. the distance from A to A, B to B, etc.
E. cancels previous sharps or flats
F. the highness or lowness of a note
G. lowers the pitch of a note by one half step

8. Write the following notes on the treble staff shown below: B, F♯, D, G, F, A, E♭, middle C.

9. Write these notes on the bass staff shown below: F, G, B♭, A, C, D♯, E.

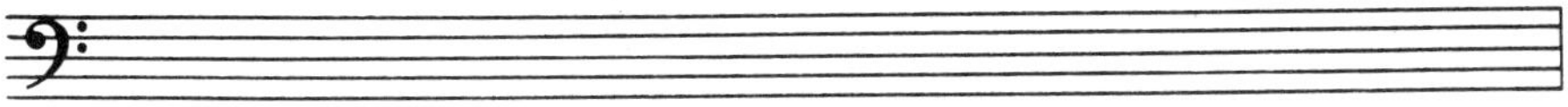

Continued in frame 195.

10. In the following space, write the names of all the notes in the melody (treble staff only) of "Billy Boy" (frame 191).

   line 1:
   line 2:
   line 3:

Identify each numbered key in the examples below by writing its name in the appropriate blank.

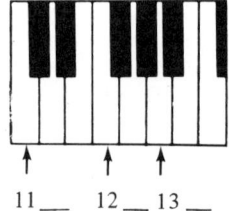

11 ___ 12 ___ 13 ___

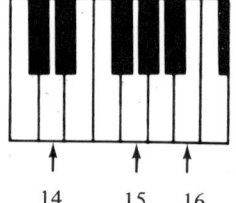

14 ___ 15 ___ 16 ___

Match the numbered black keys with the appropriate letters from the right.

17 ___ 18 ___ 19 ___

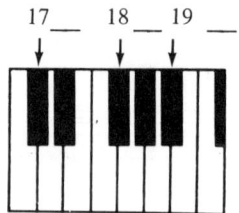

L. F-sharp or G-flat

M. C-sharp or D-flat

N. A-sharp or B-flat

Using 1/1 for whole and 1/2 for half, write the fraction that properly describes the intervals shown on this keyboard.

21 ___

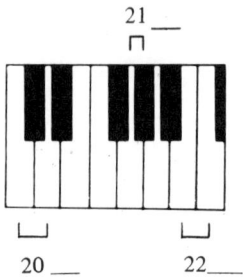

20 ___   22 ___

End of test

To grade the test, turn to frame 196.

You have now completed the Self-Test. Check your answers with the key that follows and grade your results. If you missed a substantial number of the items you probably need to read the chapter again before going on. In any case, be sure to review each of the questions you missed by looking up the material specified in parentheses next to the answer.

Answers & Review Index

1. F (pitch defined, 124)
2. D (octave defined, 175, 176)
3. A (half step defined, 158)
4. B (sharps, 162)
5. G (flats, 162)
6. E (naturals, 162)
7. C (whole step defined, 158, 164)
8.

(notes in the treble clef, 126 ff)

9.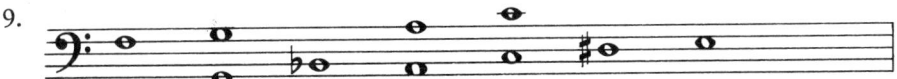

(notes in the bass clef, 138 ff)

Answers and Review Index are continued in frame 197.

10. line 1: F♯ G A A A D F♯ G A A B A F♯ G
    line 2: A A A D F♯ F♯ F♯ E E F♯
    line 3: G G G G G A G F♯ E F♯ G A D B
    line 4: A F♯ A A G E C♯ E D

11. C (piano keyboard, white keys, 144 ff)

12. F (piano keyboard, white keys, 144 ff)

13. A (piano keyboard, white keys, 144 ff)

14. D (piano keyboard, white keys, 144 ff)

15. G (piano keyboard, white keys, 144 ff)

16. B (piano keyboard, white keys, 144 ff)

17. M (piano keyboard, black keys, 167 ff)

18. L (piano keyboard, black keys, 167 ff)

19. N (piano keyboard, black keys, 167 ff)

20. 1/1 (piano keyboard, whole and half steps, 182)

21. 1/2 (piano keyboard, whole and half steps, 182)

22. 1/2 (piano keyboard, whole and half steps, 182)

4
Harmonic Structure of Music

198

In previous chapters, the basic aspects of rhythm and pitch were presented. Let us now turn our attention to the third major component of music, *harmony*. Despite differences between pieces of music, close examination of tonal combinations reveals some common and often repeated patterns. In this chapter you will become acquainted with several such patterns. There are eight Diagnostic Questions in this chapter.

Objectives

At the end of the chapter, you will be expected to do the following:

1. Recall definitions for these terms: harmony, chord, triad, and interval.
2. Identify the basic interval quantities: second, third, fourth, fifth, sixth, and seventh.
3. Recognize the difference between harmonic intervals and melodic intervals.
4. Invert any interval or chord.
5. Distinguish the quality of thirds as major or minor.
6. Determine whether a triad is major or minor.
7. Construct a triad on any given note.
8. Recognize the difference between harmonic intervals and melodic intervals.

Turn to frame 199.

199

Diagnostic Question One

Some musicians find it difficult to agree completely on a definition of *harmony* because of its complexity. Simply stated, harmony is the simultaneous sounding of at least two different tones. If three or more tones are sounded together, the result is a *chord*. When two persons sing together they are harmonizing, but not making chords.

Which of the following statements is concerned with harmony?

Alternatives

		frame
a.	The beat in that piece of music is really unusual.	205
b.	Have you ever heard anyone who could sing so high?	208
c.	When the cellos played with the violins, they played different notes.	203

200

Correct. The farther apart notes are, the larger the interval between them.

Intervals are identified by numbers. The identifying number for each interval is the number of *scale tones* included in it.

For example, in the interval C to E, there are three lines and spaces—C, D, and E—so the interval is called a *third*. This information should help you answer the next Diagnostic Question, in frame 209.

While examining the problem, remember that an interval is the distance between two notes played together or consecutively. Using the note D as a basis, here are some examples:

The bottom note is D, and the top note is E. The interval D to E encompasses only two lines and spaces and is, therefore, called a *second*.

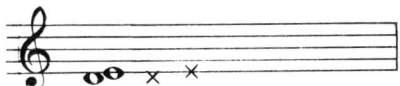

This harmonic interval has two notes: D and F. There is a line between them, namely, E. This interval encompasses *three* lines and spaces, D, E, and F. It is a *third*.

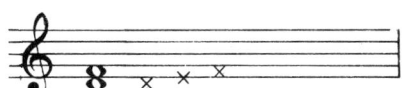

This melodic interval encompasses D (the bottom note), E, F, and G (the top note). Because it encompasses four lines and spaces, it is a *fourth*.

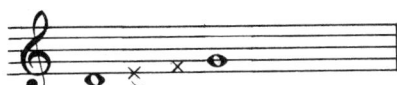

This interval is in the bass clef. The bottom note is D. The interval encompasses D, E, F, G, and A: five lines and spaces. The interval is a *fifth*.

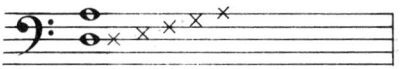

By counting an interval's bottom note and top note plus all the lines and spaces between them, you can determine the size of the interval.

Use the Shield.

What is the interval's size?

✍

It is a fourth. It encompasses F, G, A, and B—four lines and spaces.

What is the size of this interval?

✍

It is a seventh. It encompasses seven lines and spaces: F, G, A, B, C, D, and E. Please continue in frame 211.

Yes, you have selected the right inversion for each interval. One thing about inversions is consistent, and it makes them easier to work with. The graph below illustrates the point.

```
1      2      3      4      5      6      7      8
|  Second  |              Seventh                  |
```

If inverted, seconds always become sevenths, and vice versa.

```
1      2      3      4      5      6      7      8
|     Third       |            Sixth               |
```

If inverted, thirds always become sixths, and vice versa.

```
1      2      3      4      5      6      7      8
|        Fourth         |          Fifth           |
```

If inverted, fourths always become fifths, and vice versa.

The same principle can be shown on the musical staff:

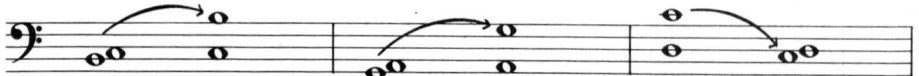

Seconds become sevenths and sevenths become seconds.

Thirds become sixths, and sixths become thirds.

Fourths become fifths, and fifths become fourths.

Turn to frame 214 for Diagnostic Question Five.

Of course. The cellos and violins are playing different notes, and that is called harmony. Now continue with the following Diagnostic Question.

Diagnostic Question Two

Another term you need to recognize is *interval*. An interval is the difference in pitch between two tones. A *harmonic interval* exists between two tones played simultaneously. In the example below, the intervals C to G and C to B are harmonic intervals. Because the distance between C to G is different than between C to B, they are different intervals. In this example, the harmonic interval between C to G is smaller than between C to B:

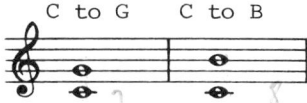

You should learn the difference between *harmonic* intervals and *melodic* intervals. Remember that a harmonic interval exists between notes that are sounded together, as illustrated in the example above. A melodic interval exists between any note and the note that immediately follows it, as illustrated below.

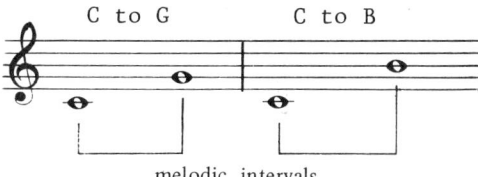

melodic intervals

Now, from the alternatives below choose the smallest and the largest intervals.

Alternatives

	Smallest		Largest	frame
a.	1	and	4	207
b.	3	and	6	200
c.	3	and	4	206

##

Not quite right. For an explanation, turn to frame 201.

##

No, that can't be right. Why? The statement you selected mentions the beat, or the pulse, of a musical selection. Beat and pulse have to do with the rhythm of music, not its harmony. Harmony is the sounding of two or more notes together, whether it involves two persons singing together or two notes played simultaneously on an instrument. Now choose the correct response in frame 199.

You are right about the smallest interval but wrong on the largest. Go to frame 207.

Because you made a mistake, please read the following explanation carefully. A harmonic interval is the difference in pitch between two notes that are played together. If you played the note

D and the note B together, the B would be

written directly above the D like this:

Those notes are farther apart than the notes D to F, if they were also played together. Look at this comparison:

Now return to the Diagnostic Question in frame 203 and see if you can answer it correctly.

208

No, that can't be right. A remark about a person's ability to sing high notes is a comment on the *range* of his voice and has nothing to do with harmony. It takes two or more simultaneous notes, sung or played, to make harmony. Now choose the correct response in frame 199.

209

Diagnostic Question Three

Choose the alternative below that correctly identifies the intervals of a *second*, *fifth*, and *sixth* in that order.

Alternatives

							frame
a.	I'm not sure. Where is the discussion on this matter?						201
	Second		Fifth		Sixth		
b.	4	and	7	and	1		204
c.	6	and	1	and	3		215
d.	6	and	2	and	1		213

210

No, you must have slipped up. For an explanation go to frame 212.

==========  ==========

Use the Shield.

Identify the size of this interval.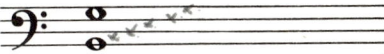

❧

It is a sixth. It covers all the lines and spaces between B and G (six).

Return to the Diagnostic Question in frame 209 and answer it correctly.

==========  ==========

It is easy to invert intervals. Simply put the bottom note of the interval on top as shown below.

In measure 1 is a fifth, E to B. By moving the bottom E *up* to the closest line or space that is still E, you invert the interval.

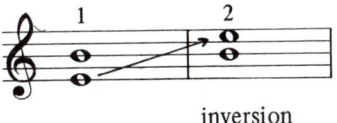

inversion

Use the Shield.

Write the inversion of this interval in the second measure.

❧

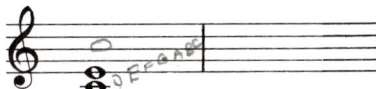

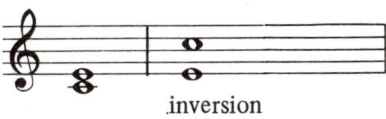

inversion

Write the inversion of this interval.

❧

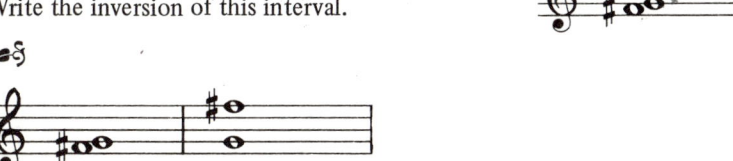

inversion

Please return to frame 213 and answer the Diagnostic Question.

Right. Now that you have identified the basic interval sizes, let's examine interval *inversions* in the following Diagnostic Question.

Diagnostic Question Four

The intervals on the left are *inversions* of which intervals on the right?

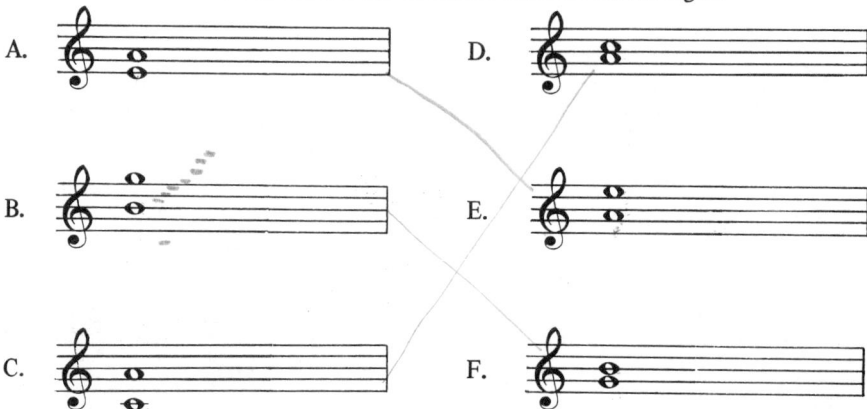

Alternatives

		frame
a.	I am not familiar with the musical meaning of inversion.	212
b.	A is the inversion of E B is the inversion of F C is the inversion of D	202
c.	A is the inversion of F B is the inversion of D C is the inversion of E	210
d.	A is the inversion of E B is the inversion of D C is the inversion of F	216

214

Diagnostic Question Five

In answering the next question and others that follow, do not guess. If you are unsure of the answer, or the process by which the answer is determined, select the first alternative and read the explanation.

Which of the following thirds are *correctly* labeled?

Alternatives

		frame
a.	I would like to read the background material before I make my choice.	218
b.	Thirds C and E are correctly labeled.	223
c.	Thirds A and D are correctly labeled.	219
d.	Thirds B and C are correctly labeled.	222

215

No, that wasn't quite right. Let's examine the problem in frame 201.

216

No, you must have made a mistake of some kind. For an explanation go to frame 212.

217

A triad is composed of two thirds (which you have already learned to identify), so learning the quality of triads will be easy.

C to E is a third. (Remember that thirds are either major or minor.) Because E is 2 whole steps above C we know the third is major.

E to G is another third. It encompasses only 1½ steps and is a minor third.

If we combine the above intervals we have a triad with a major third below a minor third. This is the makeup of a *major third*.

In this example, the bottom interval (E to G) is minor, and the top interval (G to B) is a major third. This is the makeup of a *minor triad*.

RULE: Triads contain two thirds. The quality of the *bottom* third determines the quality of the triad.

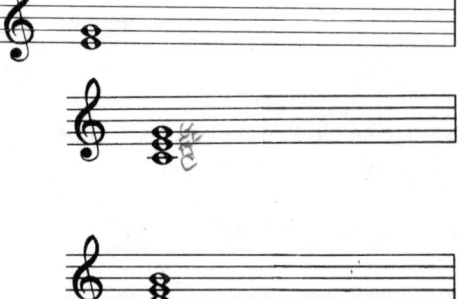

(If you need to review the material on major and minor thirds, refer to frame 218, but remember to return to this frame before you continue the program.)

Continue in frame 224.

HOW TO DISTINGUISH BETWEEN MAJOR AND MINOR THIRDS

The interval of a third is the basis of traditional Western harmony. Several intervals, including thirds, can carry the designation *major* or *minor*, terms which describe their quality. The only difference between major and minor thirds is their size. Major thirds are one half step larger than minor thirds.

C to E = major third

C to E♭ = minor third

In the example on the left, the bracket delineates a third from C to E. That interval consists of two whole steps, from C to D and from D to E. *All major thirds consist of two whole steps.* In the example on the right the bracket delineates a minor third (from C to E flat). From C to D is the first whole step, but from D to E flat is only one half step. *All minor thirds consist of 1½ steps.*

Examine the interval from A to C on the keyboard. The interval encompasses three notes (A, B, and C) and is therefore a third. From A to B is a whole step because of the key found between them. From B to C is only a half step, however, so the interval is a minor third, consisting of 1½ steps. To convert it to a major third would require changing either the A to an A flat, or the C to a C sharp.

Turn to frame 220.

That alternative was incorrect. You can find out why in frame 218.

Two more examples follow. What is the quality of this harmonic third—major or minor?

1. The interval is a third because it encompasses 3 notes: D, E, and F.
2. From D to E is a whole step. (There is a note between them on the keyboard.)
3. From E to F is only a half step.
   ANSWER: The interval is a minor third because it encompasses 1½ steps.

What is the quality of this melodic third—major or minor?

1. The interval is a third because it encompasses 3 notes: E flat, F, and G.
2. From E flat to F is a whole step. (There is a note between them.)
3. From F to G is a whole step.

ANSWER: The interval is a major third because it encompasses 2 steps.

Turn to frame 221.

221

Use the Shield.

Are there two whole steps in this interval?

No, there are 1½ steps; F to G and G to A flat.

If there are 1½ steps in the interval above, is it a major or minor third?

Minor. Major thirds need two whole steps.

Please identify this interval as major or minor.

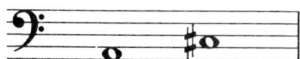

It is major. From A to B is a whole step and from B to C sharp is a whole step.

Please return to the Diagnostic Question in frame 214.

222

The answer you selected was incorrect. Let's see why. Turn to frame 218.

223

You are right. A minor third is smaller than a major third by one half step.

Now continue with the following Diagnostic Question.

Diagnostic Question Six*

If three notes of a chord fall on consecutive lines or consecutive spaces, the chord formed is called a *triad*, an important musical unit.

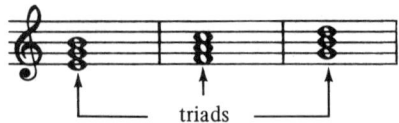
triads

By identifying the nature of the intervals of a triad, you can also determine whether the triad itself is major or minor.

Is the triad below major or minor?

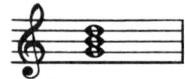

Alternatives

		frame
a.	I'm not sure. I would like an explanation.	217
b.	major	226
c.	minor	228

*If you have answered this question before, answer it correctly again and proceed with the program.

224

Use the Shield.

In this example, the bottom third is major, the top third is minor. Is the triad major or minor?

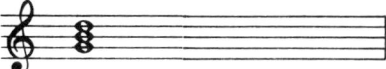

major

Is this triad major or minor?

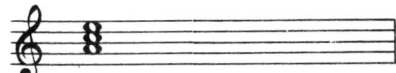

minor (The bottom third is minor.)

What two intervals make up a *minor* triad?

A minor third in the bottom interval, and a major third in the top interval.

Is this triad major or minor?

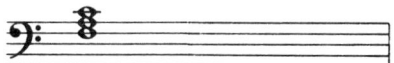

major (The bottom interval is major.)

Now return to the Diagnostic Question in frame 223.

225

Were you misled by the fact that those three chords all had the same notes, except for the sharp and flat? Please read the explanation in frame 231.

226

Yes, the chord is a major triad. If the notes of a chord fall on three consecutive lines or spaces, it is a triad. A triad is made up of a bottom interval (a third) and a top interval (a third). If the bottom third is major, the triad is major. If the bottom third is minor, the triad is minor.

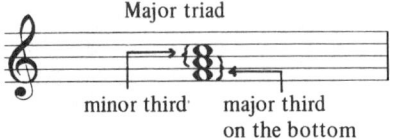

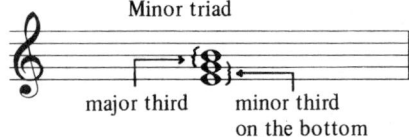

Now try the following Diagnostic Question.

Diagnostic Question Seven

Which of the following triads are major?

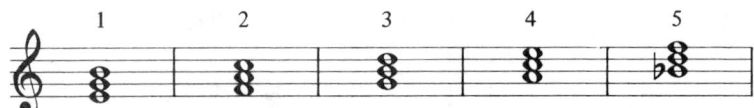

Alternatives

		frame
a.	May I review this concept?	217
b.	1 and 4 are major.	230
c.	3 and 5 are major.	232
d.	2 and 5 are major.	229

Use the Shield.

Which chord on the right is in root position?

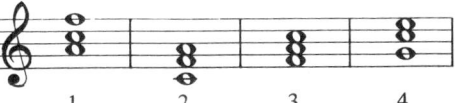

Chord number 3 is in root position.

Which of those chords is a first inversion of chord number 3?

Chord number 1 is the first inversion of chord number 3.

Which of those chords is *not* an inversion of the others?

Chord number 4 is a C major triad, second inversion. All others are inversions of the F major triad.

This chord is an inversion. Write the chord in its root position in the second measure.

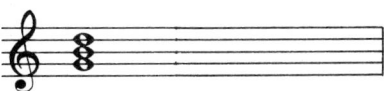

Here is a root position triad. Write its first inversion in the next measure.

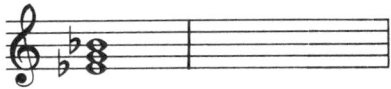

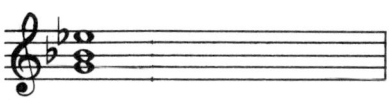

Turn to frame 229.

228

You chose the wrong alternative. You will find out why by reading the review in frame 217.

229

Exactly. You have learned to identify some major and minor triads. Although many other chords exist in music, our discussion is limited to these important basic ones.

Diagnostic Question Eight

Of the chords shown below, three are related by being a root chord and its two inversions. Which are they?

Alternatives

		frame
a.	I'm not sure of the meaning of inversion as applied to this example. Please explain.	231
b.	Chords 1, 2, and 4.	225
c.	Chords 1, 3, and 5.	233

You have made an error. An explanation of the concept can be found in frame 217.

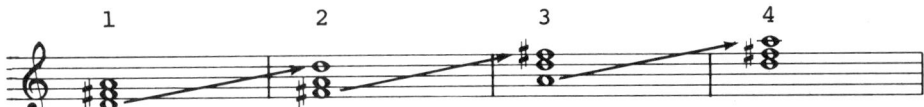

This Diagnostic Question tested your knowledge of chord inversions.

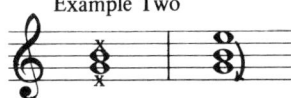

When a chord is built on three consecutive lines or spaces we call it a triad. We may also say it is in *root* position (see measure 1 above). By moving the bottom note of the chord (in this case, D) to the top of the chord, the chord becomes a *first inversion*, as illustrated in measure 2. If you invert it again by moving the new bottom note to the top, you create a *second inversion* (measure 3). If you repeat the process still another time, you are back in root position again, but *one octave higher* than the original position.

All triads can exist in these three different positions. To determine whether any chord is a triad, however, you must return it to root position to see if it actually does fall on consecutive lines or spaces.

How can the chord on the right be arranged on three consecutive lines or spaces and therefore qualify as a triad?

Example One

ANSWER: By examining the chord in Example 1, you will see that two of the notes are already on consecutive lines. These two notes are shown in Example 2. If three consecutive lines are to be used, either the line below the two (see the bottom X) or the line above (see the top X) must be employed. The top note in Example 1 is an E, the same note as the bottom X in Example 2. When it is moved down you have a triad.

Example Two

Turn to frame 227.

232

You seem to be confused about something. A review begins in frame 217.

233

Correct. The chords you chose were inversions of one another. Triads exist in *root position,* *first inversion,* and *second inversion* as shown below.

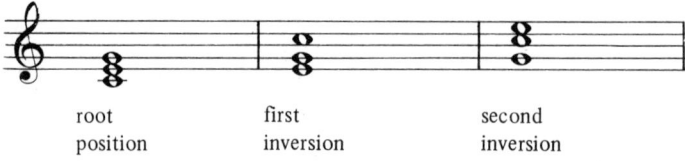

       root   first   second
    position   inversion   inversion

Congratulations! You have now completed Chapter 4. You will find several helpful *Skill Builders* on the following pages. Be sure to do them. They will help refine the knowledge you have just acquired.

Please go to the next frame.

234

♦ **THE NEXT STEP...**

This part of the program explores two things: (1) the quality of intervals other than thirds, and (2) a different process for determining the quality of all intervals. You may read it if you wish. If not, the Skill Builders begin in frame 238.

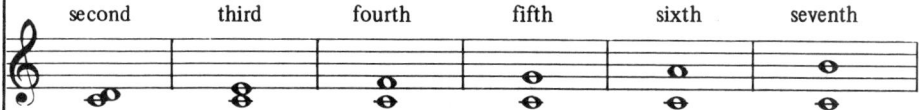

The example above includes intervals of a second, third, fourth, fifth, sixth, and seventh. You have learned that thirds are either major or minor. That is also true of seconds, sixths, and sevenths. Each of these intervals may be designated major or minor.

Fourths and fifths are different. The standard fourth or fifth is designated *perfect.* If a perfect interval is increased by one half step it is said to be *augmented.* If it is decreased by one half step it is *diminished.*

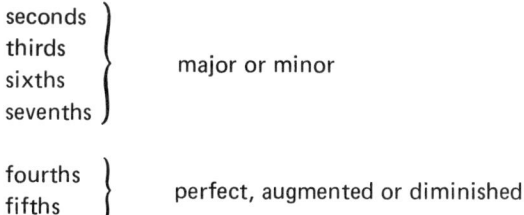

Please turn to the next frame.

ANOTHER WAY TO DISTINGUISH BETWEEN MAJOR AND MINOR THIRDS

The interval of a third is the basis of traditional Western harmony. Remember, thirds can be designated major or minor, with the major third being one half step larger than the minor third. The terms *major* and *minor* define the *quality* of an interval. (Its *size* is the numerical designation, second, third, fourth, and so on.) Determining the quality of an interval involves a high-level thought process that takes some effort at first, but with time becomes as easy as multiplication tables.

Here is a three-step process for determining the quality of a third. It is the process followed by many musicians in determining the quality of any interval. Follow the steps carefully.

1. Assume for the moment that the bottom note of the interval is the first note of the major scale beginning on that note. In this example, the bottom note is G, so assume the G-major scale.

2. Identify the key signature for that scale. (If you don't know the key signature, look it up in frame 394.) The key signature for G major is one sharp, F♯.

3. With the key signature fixed, we are ready to determine the quality of the third. *If the top note of the third belongs to that major scale, it is a major third.* In our example, the interval is major, because the top note (B) is naturally part of the G-major scale.

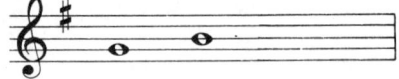

Two more examples of the process are given below:

What is the quality of this harmonic third—major or minor?

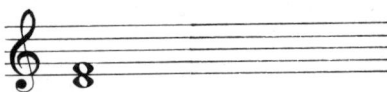

1. Assume the bottom note (D) begins the D-major scale.

2. Ascertain the key signature of D major: two sharps, F♯ and C♯.

3. Is the top note of the interval (F) in the D-major scale?

Please turn to frame 236.

ANSWER: No; the D-major scale employs an F♯. The top note of the interval is an F-natural, which is one half step lower. The interval is, therefore, a *minor* third.

What is the quality of this melodic third—major or minor?

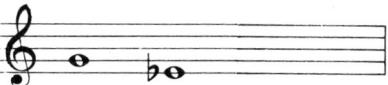

1. Assume the bottom note of this interval (E♭) begins the E♭-major scale.
2. What is the key signature of E♭ major? Three flats: B♭, E♭, A♭.
3. Is the top note of the interval (G) in the E♭-major scale?

   ANSWER: Yes, G falls naturally in the E♭-major scale, so the interval is a *major* third.

Now, try some exercises in major and minor thirds.

Use the Shield.

Please identify this interval as major or minor.

The bottom note of the interval indicates we will employ which major scale?

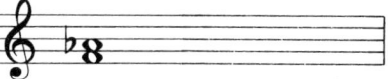

F major

What is the key signature for F major?

One flat, B♭

Does the top note (A♭) of this third fall naturally in the F-major scale?

No, in the F-major scale there is an A natural. Our interval is one half step smaller, so the interval is a minor third.

Please turn to frame 237.

- Use the illustration to identify this third as major or minor.

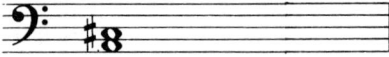

What scale will we employ in this bass clef example?

☙

A-major scale because the bottom note is A

What is the key signature for A-major?

☙

Three sharps, F♯, C♯, G♯

Is the C♯ (top note of the interval) in the A-major scale?

☙

Yes, one of the sharps in the key signature is C♯.

Is the interval major or minor in quality?

☙

It is a major third, because the top note of the interval is in the A-major scale.

The process of determining the quality of thirds is somewhat complicated, but it has very wide applicability. Not only can you determine the quality of thirds, but the method works for all intervals of the octave.

If you assume the bottom note of the interval is the first note of that major scale:

Seconds, thirds, sixths, and *sevenths* are major if they occur naturally in the scale. If they are one half step less than the major scale tone, the intervals will be minor.

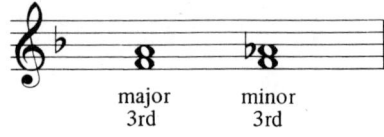

major 3rd   minor 3rd

Fourths and *fifths* are perfect if they occur naturally in the scale.

- You now have the capability of determining the quality of any interval in music through this one process. As you gain experience with the sounds of the intervals, their different sound qualities will be of additional assistance.

The Skill Builders begin on the next page.

Skill Builders

1. Five intervals are shown below. Draw the inversion of each in the empty measures provided.

   A. 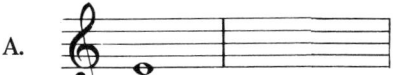   D.

   B. 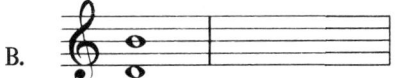   E.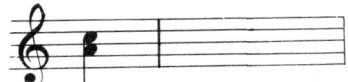

   C.

2. Shown below are several intervals of a third. Determine the quality (major or minor) of each interval. You may review the process in frame 218 if needed.

3. In the measures shown below, construct a major triad on each of the notes given.

4. Using the triads you just made as your model, write either the first inversion or the second inversion of each one, and label it correctly.

   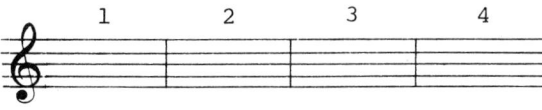

5. Return to the triads in number 3 and change them to minor triads by reducing the size of the bottom third one half step.

Turn to frame 239.

AMERICA THE BEAUTIFUL

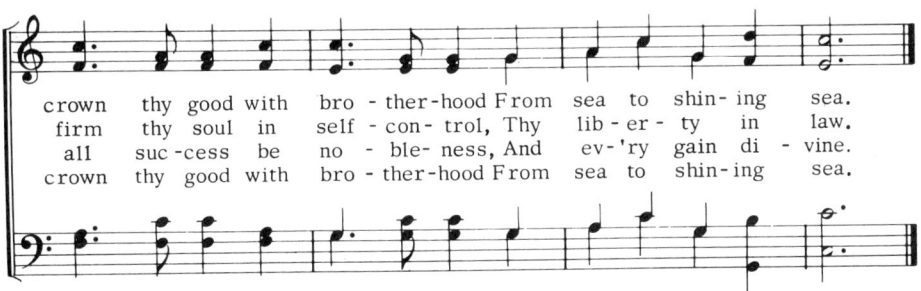

6. Practice singing the melody of "America the Beautiful" by yourself. If possible, play the first note on an instrument so you can sing it at the pitch in which it is written.

7. Practice harmony by singing the alto, tenor, or bass part of "America the Beautiful" several times. You may need to play the part slowly on an instrument to help you learn it.

8. Sing the melody of the song, "Cockles and Mussels" several times, and have a partner sing the alto part. Then sing it together and enjoy the pleasant harmonies it contains. Try playing one hand (or both) on the piano.

9. In the song "Cockles and Mussels" on the next page, point at different intervals in the song at random and identify their sizes. If the interval is a third, identify its quality as well.

Turn to the next frame.

241

COCKLES AND MUSSELS

Irish folksong

1. In Dublin's fair city Where girls are so pretty, 'Twas there I first saw my sweet Molly Malone; She wheeled a wheelbarrow 'Thro streets broad and narrow, Crying "Cockles and mussels! Alive, alive, oh!"
2. She was a fishmonger, But it was no wonder, For so were her father and mother before; They each wheeled a barrow 'Thro streets broad and narrow, Crying "Cockles and mussels! Alive, alive, oh!"
3. She died of a fever And nothing could save her, And that was the end of sweet Molly Malone; Her ghost wheels a barrow 'Thro streets broad and narrow, Crying "Cockles and mussels! Alive, alive, oh!"

Chorus: "Alive, alive, oh! Alive, alive, oh!" Crying "Cockles and mussels! Alive, alive, oh!"

10. Look at the song, "The Magic of Christmas," (frame 242). Can you find any melodic thirds in the melody? Circle them. What harmonic intervals are most common in the accompaniment? Try singing or playing the melody. Then sing it as a round.

Turn to the next frame.

*Used with permission, A. Laurence Lyon, Oregon College of Education, Monmouth, Oregon.

11. In "Reuben and Rachel," the note D has been written in the bass clef for each measure. Using that note as the lowest note in each chord, write the following triad in each measure:

measure 1: D major triad, root position
measure 2: G major triad, second inversion
measure 3: D major triad, root position
measure 4: G major triad, second inversion, then D major triad, root position
measure 5: D major triad, root position
measure 6: G major triad, second inversion
measure 7: D major triad, root position
measure 8: G major triad, second inversion, then D major triad, root position

REUBEN AND RACHEL

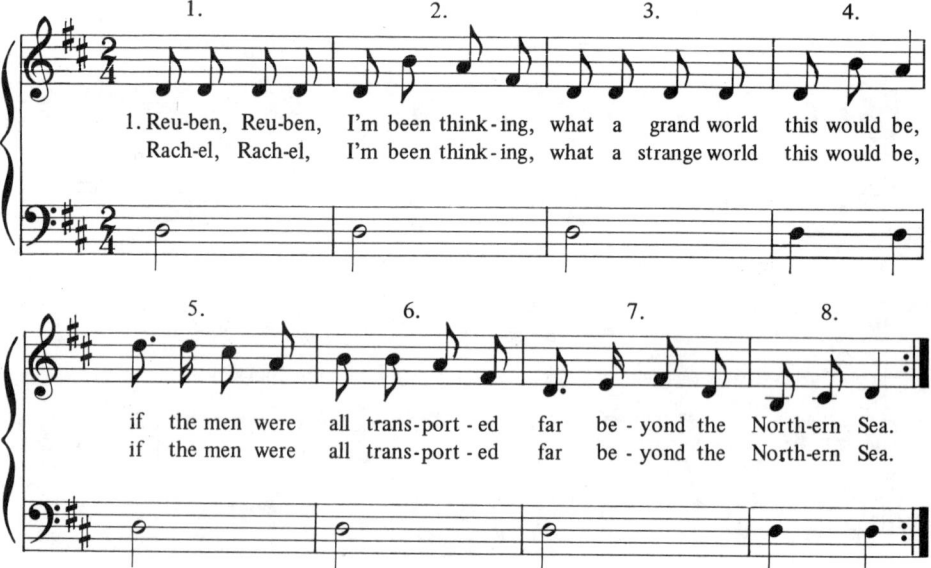

Verse 2. Reuben, Reuben, I've been thinking, If we did cross o'er the seas,
All the men would follow after, like a swarm of bumble bees.

Verse 3. Reuben, Reuben, I've been thinking, Life would be so easy then,
What a lovely world we'd have—, If there were no tiresome men.

Verse 4. Reuben, Reuben, stop your teasing, If indeed you do love me,
I was only just a foolin', As I thought that you would see.

The Self-Test is found in the next frame.

Self-Test

You are now ready to evaluate your understanding of the material in Chapter 4, so you can determine the concepts to review. When considering intervals, you may use the keyboard on the shield if you so desire.

Match the three terms with the proper definition on the right.

1. chord _____
2. harmony _____
3. interval _____
4. triad _____

A. a chord with the notes placed on three consecutive lines or spaces

B. any combination of notes that are sounded together

C. the difference in pitch between two notes played simultaneously or consecutively

D. three or more tones sounded together

Identify each interval on the staff below by writing its size (i.e., second, third, fourth, etc.) underneath.

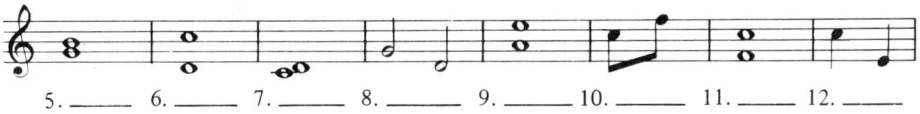

5. _____ 6. _____ 7. _____ 8. _____ 9. _____ 10. _____ 11. _____ 12. _____

Identify the intervals on the staff below as major or minor thirds and write your answers underneath.

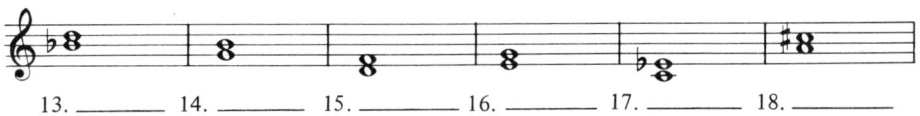

13. _____ 14. _____ 15. _____ 16. _____ 17. _____ 18. _____

19. These two intervals are the same in all ways but one. How are they different?

20. What two intervals are necessary to create a major triad?
    A _____ below a _____

21. What two intervals are necessary to create a minor triad?
    A _____ below a _____

Turn to the next frame.

Identify each of the following triads as major or minor.

22 _____   23 _____   24 _____   25 _____

Construct a triad on each note on the staff. Then write its first inversion in the next measure.

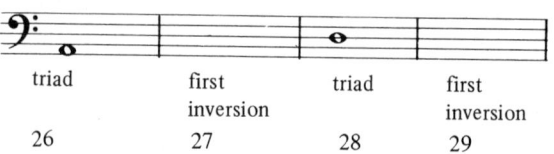

triad   first   triad   first
        inversion   inversion
26   27   28   29

30. In "America the Beautiful" (frame 239), how many harmonic intervals of a third are there in the treble clef? How many in the bass clef?
    treble: _____   bass: _____

Three intervals are shown below. Invert each interval and write the result at the appropriate place on the staff.

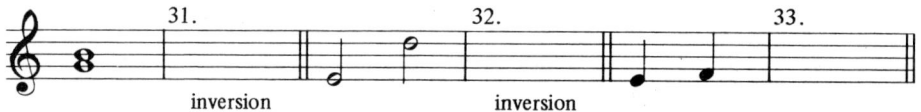

31.   32.   33.
inversion   inversion

You have completed the Self-Test. Now check your answers on the following page.

246

Check your answers with those in the key that follows. Be sure to review all missed questions immediately by referring to the part indicated in the Review Index. If you missed a substantial number of questions you probably need to review the chapter. Go through it again, carefully choosing your answers to the Diagnostic Questions. Then go on to Chapter 5, frame 248.

Answers & Review Index

1. D (chord defined, 199)
2. B (harmony defined, 199)
3. C (interval defined, 203)
4. A (triad defined, 223)
5. 3rd (interval size, 201)
6. 7th (interval size, 201)
7. 2nd (interval size, 201)
8. 4th (interval size, 201)
9. 5th (interval size, 201)
10. 4th (interval size, 201)
11. 5th (interval size, 201)
12. 6th (interval size, 201)
13. major third (quality of thirds, 218 ff)
14. major third (quality of thirds, 218 ff)
15. minor third (quality of thirds, 218 ff)
16. minor third (quality of thirds, 218 ff)
17. minor third (quality of thirds, 218 ff)
18. major third (quality of thirds, 218 ff)
19. The first measure is a *harmonic* interval, the second is a *melodic* interval (harmonic and melodic intervals, 203)
20. A major third below a minor third (quality of triads, 217)
21. A minor third below a major third (quality of triads, 217)

Continued in frame 247.

22. major (quality of triads, 217)
23. minor (quality of triads, 217)
24. major (quality of triads, 217)
25. major (quality of triads, 217 ff)

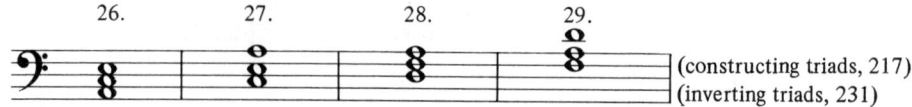

30. Treble clef: 25 thirds; base clef: 5 thirds (interval size, 201)

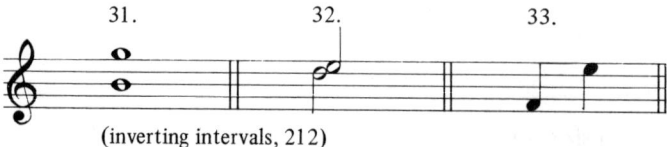

(inverting intervals, 212)

5
Major Scales, Chords, and Keys

248

For many years, traditional Western music has been dominated by a system of harmony known as *tertian*, i.e., based on the interval of a third. An understanding of tertian harmony requires knowledge of scales, chords, keys, and key tones—the subjects of this chapter.

Objectives

1. Recognize definitions of key, key tone, scale, and tonality.
2. Recall at what places in major scales the half steps are located.
3. Recall some characteristic relationships of the notes of the major scale, particularly notes 1, 2, 5, and 7.
4. Recall the syllabic names of the notes in the solfege system, and begin using it with simple songs.
5. Determine key signatures by using a "circle of fifths" diagram.
6. Demonstrate knowledge of the keys of C, G, D, F, and B flat as follows:

    Concerning the scale of each key:

    a. Illustrate where the half steps fall in each scale.
    b. Recognize the key signature for each key.
    c. Identify the structurally important notes in each scale by name.

    Concerning chords in each key:

    a. Recognize the names of the primary chords.
    b. Identify some major characteristics of the I, IV, and V chords.
    c. Recall possible substitutes for the I, IV, and V chords.

7. Determine the seventh note that makes a V chord a V_7 chord.

Turn to frame 249.

To discuss tertian harmony intelligently you must understand these musical concepts:

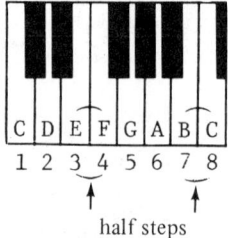

C-major scale

A *scale* is a series of notes within any octave (e.g., C to C or D to D) that follows a particular arrangement of whole and half steps. The effect of the arrangement is to give one tone dominance over the others so that they seem to be "pulled" toward it. If you count the first note in the octave as number 1 and give each named note—in order of ascending pitch—the numbers 2 to 8, major scales will have half steps between steps 3 to 4 and 7 to 8. (See the example above.) All other steps are whole steps.

In other words, a major scale consists of eight notes within an octave arranged in a set pattern of whole steps and half steps. The half steps lie between steps 3 to 4 and 7 to 8.

1. *Key*: a system of tones that are drawn to a central tone, and bear the name of the central tone (e.g., key of F).

2. *Key Tone*: the central tone to which other tones are drawn; where complete resolution is found.

3. *Scale*: a series of tones in ascending or descending order, beginning with the key tone, and maintaining fixed distances between all tones.

4. *Tonality*: the organization of tones around a key tone.

Before proceeding with this chapter, be sure you understand these definitions. They will be required of you later in the program. There are eight Diagnostic Questions in this chapter.

Turn to the next frame.

250

Diagnostic Question One

In the key of C, the key tone is C; in the key of D, it is D, and so on. The key tone is always the first (1) and last (8) tone of any scale. Beginning with the key tone, the notes of the scale are numbered 1 through 8 in ascending order.

From the alternatives below, choose the one that correctly matches the tone with its number *in the key of* G *major*. (You may use the keyboard facsimile on the back of the book.)

Alternatives

		frame
a.	Could I see the review before selecting an answer?	252
b.	D = 5, C = 4, G = 1, E = 6	255
c.	D = 2, C = 1, G = 5, E = 3	254
d.	D = 4, C = 3, G = 1, E = 6	257

251

Did you misunderstand the question? In any event you need to give some more thought to the formation of a major scale. Please go to frame 260.

252

Here is the review. When numbering the tones in any scale, give the key tone the first number. For the key of G, the key tone is G. For the key of F, it is F. Using the key of F as an example, the notes of the F-major scale are numbered as follows, with every letter name receiving a number:

F G A B♭ C D E F
1 2 3 4 5 6 7 8

If you examine the intervals between steps 3 to 4 and 7 to 8 on a keyboard you will see that a flat must be added to the B to make a major scale. However, that addition does not affect the position (or numbers) of the notes within the scale.

Use the Shield.

In the key of A major, what are the numbers of D, F♯, and G♯?

4, 6, 7: A B C♯ D E F♯ G♯ A
         1 2 3 4 5 6 7 8

In the key of F major, what are the numbers of notes, G, A, and E?

2, 3, 7: F G A B♭ C D E F
         1 2 3 4 5 6 7 8

In the key of D major, what numbers are notes E, G, and A?

2, 4, 5: D E F♯ G A B C♯ D

Return to the question in frame 250.

253

Not quite. You forgot one important detail. To brush up on this subject turn to frame 260.

254

No, let's look at the problem again. Turn to frame 252.

255

Precisely. In the G-major scale (or any other scale), tone 1 falls on the key tone and the other tones follow in order. The numbers of the scale are sometimes referred to as *scale degrees*.

G A B C D E F♯ G
scale degrees — 1 2 3 4 5 6 7 8

SCALE TONE TENDENCIES

The definition of a key tone stated that other tones in the key are drawn toward that tone. This is true with different degrees of intensity for different tones. The key tone (tone 1 or 8) is the most important tone, where the aural sense of conclusion or "arrival" is achieved. Tone 7 is strongly drawn up to tone 8. Tone 2 is likewise drawn down to tone 1.

1 2 3 4 5 6 7 8

Tone 7 is drawn to 8 with greater intensity than any other tone. One reason for this effect is that it is just one half step from the key tone and very much under its influence.

Because of Western musical tradition (and acoustical reasons that will not be discussed here), the fifth tone of the scale is used as the main point of departure from the key tone and is the second most important tone in the scale. Tone 5 may resolve with equal ease either up to tone 8 or down to tone 1 (as shown below), falling a fifth to 1, or jumping a fourth to 8.

1 2 3 4 5 6 7 8

Other tones in the scale also tend to follow certain patterns of progression (e.g., tone 4 tends toward tone 3), but the tones of main importance are those mentioned and illustrated in the preceding diagram.

Go to frame 256.

256

Use the Shield.

In the D-major scale (shown below), the note E will tend to resolve to note _____, and C-sharp will tend to resolve to _____.

D E F♯ G A B C♯ D

D (1) and D (8)

In the D-major scale, what is the name of the fifth tone that can jump down to 1 or up to 8 equally well?

A

In any major scale, the second tone tends to resolve (*up/down*) and the seventh tone tends to resolve (*up/down*).

down, up

The fifth tone is the second most important note of the scale; only the first tone is more important. The fifth tone is the main point of departure in the scale and resolves (*up to 8/down to 1*)

Both! The fifth tone may resolve either direction.

Go to frame 258.

257

Oops, let's look again. Go to frame 252.

258

Diagnostic Question Two

In the beginning paragraphs of this chapter, a major scale was said to have whole steps between all notes of the scale except two, which are half steps. In the scale of G major (beginning and ending on G), the *half* steps will fall between which tones?

G-major scale

Alternatives

		frame
a.	I'm not sure. Please explain further.	260
b.	B-sharp to C and F-sharp to G	251
c.	B to C and F to G	253
d.	B to C and F-sharp to G	262

259

You are right. Turn to frame 268 for the next Diagnostic Question.

All right, let's take a more detailed look at the major scale.

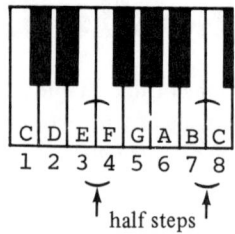
C-major scale

We are using the C-major scale to observe where the half steps fall in a major scale because it shows the half steps without using black keys. All other major scales use some black keys to get the half steps in the right places. Remember: *All major scales have half steps between notes 3 to 4 and 7 to 8 of the ascending scale.*

You can form a major scale in any octave by numbering the notes 1 through 8, as we did above, and putting half steps in the designated places, making sure all letter names of the scale are used. For example:

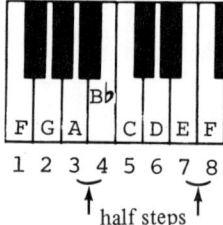
F-major scale

B♭ is needed here to create the half step from 3 to 4. (A half step already exists between E and F.)

Here is another example:

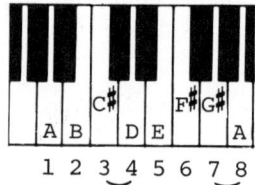
A-major scale

Sharps are needed here to create the major-scale pattern of whole steps and half steps.

Go to frame 261.

261

Use the Shield.

If you number the notes in this scale, the lower G will be note number 1 and B will be note number _____.

3

Every step in the major scale is a whole step except the steps 3–4 and _____.

7–8

The steps 3–4 and 7–8 are (*whole/half*) steps.

half

Steps 3 and 4 in the G-major scale fall on notes ____ and ____.

B, C

Steps 7 and 8 fall on notes ____ and ____ in the G-major scale.

F♯, G

Now return to frame 258 and see if you can answer the Diagnostic Question correctly.

262

Correct. The half steps fall between steps 3–4 and 7–8, or B–C and F♯–G in G major.

Now turn to frame 263.

263

Diagnostic Question Three

Now see if you can find half steps 3 to 4 and 7 to 8 in the key of F major. (Remember to keep all other intervals whole steps.)

When you have found them, choose the alternative below that correctly lists the half steps:

Alternatives

		frame
a.	I'm still unsure.	265
b.	B to C and E to F	269
c.	B-flat to C and F-sharp to G	267
d.	A to B-flat and E to F	259

264

That is right.

C major has no sharps or flats:

G major has one sharp (F♯):

F major has one flat (B♭):

Turn to frame 273.

265

All right, let's examine the key of F major step by step.

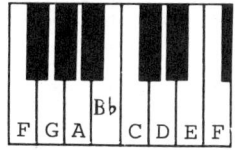
F major

First, number the notes from 1 to 8, beginning with the first note of the scale. For F major, begin on F, just as for G major you began on G. Note number 8, the last one, should have the same letter name as note number 1.

Since you are looking for half steps on 3 to 4 and 7 to 8, you now look for the notes which have the appropriate numbers. Steps 3 and 4 are A and B; 7 and 8 are E and F.

The next step is to make sure that steps 3 to 4 and 7 to 8 are half steps—that there are no keys between them—and all other intervals are whole steps. Since step 3 to 4 is A to B, there is a black key between them. An adjustment is needed. If you substitute B-flat for B, the step becomes a half step and the other intervals remain whole steps. F major will, therefore, always use B-flat instead of B for its fourth step. Step 7 to 8 is E to F—a half step as it stands—so no adjustment is needed there.

Return now to answer the Diagnostic Question in frame 263.

266

That wasn't quite right. Please continue in frame 274.

267

You have chosen the wrong alternative. Please read the explanation in frame 265.

268

Diagnostic Question Four

Rather than continually writing and rewriting the sharps or flats before the notes that require them in a particular key, musicians long ago devised a system of grouping the sharps and flats next to the meter signature. Such a group is called the *key signature*. Several signatures are shown below.

A key signature may be defined as a group of sharps or flats appearing at the beginning of each staff of music to indicate the key of the music. Key signatures show the performer what notes in the scale must be altered so that all steps of the scale are whole steps except steps 3 to 4 and 7 to 8, which are half steps. Just as a meter signature establishes the beat, key signatures establish the key of the music. Match the examples on the left with the proper key on the right.

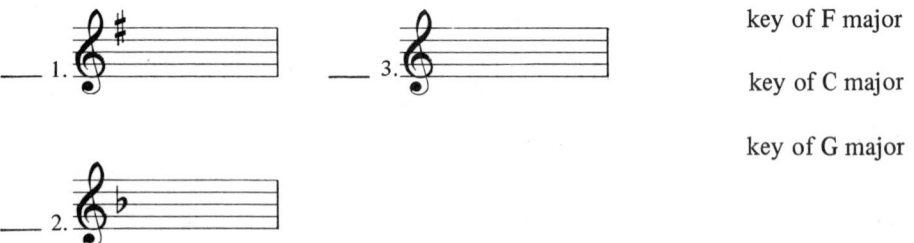

Alternatives

		frame
a.	I need an explanation before attempting to answer this question.	270
b.	1 = key of C major 3 = key of G major 2 = key of F major	275
c.	1 = key of G major 3 = key of C major 2 = key of F major	264
d.	1 = key of F major 3 = key of C major 2 = key of G major	272

No, you have chosen the wrong answer. Please read frame 265.

O.K., read the following carefully. Earlier you learned that the key of G major would always need an F-sharp to provide the half step between 7 and 8. The key signature for G major, therefore, is F-sharp, as shown on the right.

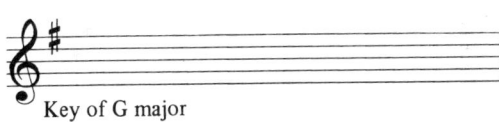

We determined that F major would always need a B-flat to locate the half step between 3 and 4 properly. F major will, therefore, always use B-flat for its key signature.

We know that C major has no sharps or flats; therefore, the key signature for C major has no sharps or flats.

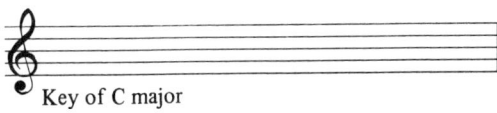

When sharps or flats are placed in a key signature, those notes will be altered *every time they appear* in the music. No reminder is needed near the note itself.

Turn to frame 271.

Use the Shield.

Which key signatures do we need to learn?

☙

C major, F major, and G major

Which one has no sharps or flats?

☙

C major

The key of G major needs how many sharps or flats?

☙

one sharp, F♯

Does the key of F major need sharps or flats?

☙

yes, flats

Which ones?

☙

only one flat, B♭

Put the Shield Aside.

Now write the names of the sharps or flats needed in each of the following key signatures.

C major =   F major =   G major =

These key signatures correctly establish all the intervals (as whole steps or half steps) in the scale, eliminating the need to write the accidentals (sharps or flats) on the staff each time the note appears.

Please return to frame 268 and answer the Diagnostic Question.

That alternative was incorrect. A brief review should clear up your problem. Go to frame 270.

Diagnostic Question Five

Pictured below are three key signatures. Identify each and choose the correct alternative.

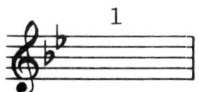  

Alternatives

		frame
a.	I am unsure of this concept. Please explain.	274
b.	1 = A major 2 = B♭ major 3 = D major	266
c.	1 = D major 2 = A major 3 = B♭ major	276
d.	1 = B♭ major 2 = D major 3 = A major	279

By now it must be apparent that there are many major keys and scales. The diagram below is known as a *circle of fifths*. It depicts all major scales and the number of sharps or flats in each of their key signatures. If you begin at the top and follow around the right side of the circle, you will see that each new key is the interval of a fifth above the previous key, and adds one sharp to the previous key signature. Going the opposite direction, each new key adds one flat. At the bottom, several keys are labeled *enharmonic keys*, because they consist of exactly the same tones, but the notes are identified by different names.

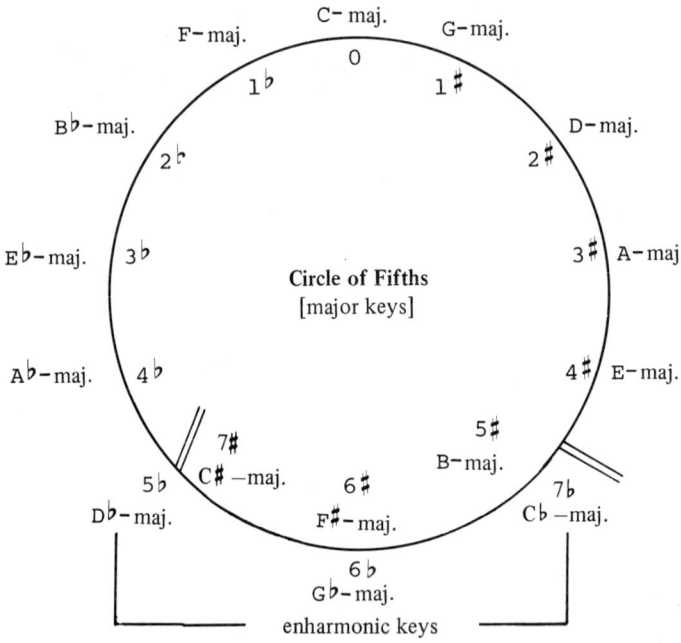

IMPORTANT: In any key signature involving sharps, the sharps always appear in the following order: F♯, C♯, G♯, D♯, A♯, E♯, B♯. For example:

—If the key signature is 1♯, it will always be F♯.

—If the key signature is 2♯, they will always be F♯ and C♯.

—If the key signature is 3♯, they will always be F♯, C♯, and G♯. And so on, through all seven sharps.

Likewise, in key signatures involving flats, the flats always appear in the following order: B♭, E♭, A♭, D♭, G♭, C♭, F♭.

Many people feel it is important to memorize the order of sharps and flats because it helps them determine key signatures.

Please turn to frame 277.

275

You have mixed up two of the key signatures. Go to frame 270.

276

That wasn't quite right. Go to frame 274.

There is an easy way to figure out keys from their signatures. It is much easier to remember than trying to memorize all the key signatures and their names.

FLATS: Reading *from left to right*, the next to last flat in the signature bears the name of the key. (Example 1 indicates the key of E-flat. Example 2 indicates the key of B-flat.)

SHARPS: Reading *from left to right*, the key note is one half step above the last sharp in the signature. (Example 3 indicates the key of E major, and Example 4 indicates the key of A major.)

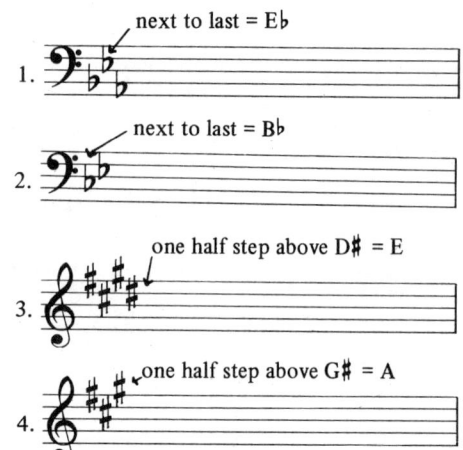

Here are two more examples. In Example 5, the next to last flat is A-flat; the key is A-flat major. In Example 6, the last sharp is A-sharp; the note directly above A-sharp is B, so the key is B major.

Now turn to frame 278.

It is not necessary to recognize all key signatures and remember their names, although this ability is beneficial. It is important, however, to be able to determine key signatures by applying the procedures discussed in frame 277 (or by looking them up in the circle of fifths, frame 274). Using one of those methods, answer the following questions.

Use the Shield.

What key does this signature indicate?

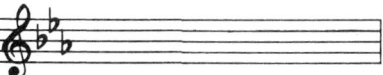

E♭ major

What key does this signature indicate?

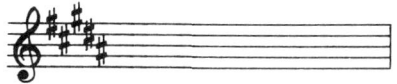

B major

What key signature has four sharps?

E major

What key signature has five flats?

D♭ major

What key signature has two sharps?

D major

Now return to the question in frame 273.

You're right. It is not always desirable to look up key signatures in the circle of fifths, so the most frequently used ones should be committed to memory as soon as possible. (All key signatures and scales are shown in the Appendix at the end of the book.)

Use the Shield.

The B-flat major key signature consists of how many flats?

☙

two (B-flat and E-flat)

The A-major key signature consists of how many sharps or flats?

☙

three sharps (F-sharp, C-sharp, and G-sharp)

The key signature for D major consists of how many sharps or flats?

☙

two sharps (F-sharp and C-sharp)

A major has three sharps. They are _____, _____, and _____.

☙

F-sharp, C-sharp, and G-sharp

D major has two sharps. They are _____ and _____.

☙

F-sharp and C-sharp

A major has the same sharps as D major plus one more, namely, _____.

☙

G-sharp

In B-flat major, the two flats are _____ and _____.

☙

B-flat, E-flat

Turn to frame 280.

280

It may be necessary to use a piano keyboard to determine the following answers. It will certainly be necessary to remember which sharps or flats are included in the keys under consideration.

Use the Shield.

In the key of A major, note names 1, 4, and 5 are _____, _____, and _____.

🖎

A, D, E

In B-flat major, notes 1, 4, and 5 are _____, _____, and _____.

🖎

B-flat, E-flat, F

In D major, notes 2, 3, and 7 are _____, _____, and _____.

🖎

E, F-sharp, C-sharp

In B-flat major, notes 2, 3, and 7 are _____, _____, and _____.

🖎

C, D, A

In A major, notes 2, 5, and 7 are _____, _____, and _____.

🖎

B, E, G-sharp

In any scale the most important tone is number _____, and the second most important tone is _____.

🖎

Tone 1 is most important, and 5 is next in importance.

Go to frame 281.

TONIC SOL-FA SYSTEM

Many musicians prefer to give the tones of the scale syllabic names rather than numbers because syllables are much easier to sing. This system of syllables, known as the *tonic sol-fa*, or *movable do*, system, has been widely used for many years. Most children become acquainted with the symbols in grade school. The names of the notes are identified below. (The scale is usually read from the bottom up, and may seem most familiar to you that way.)

Scale Number	Syllable
8	Do
7	Ti
6	La
5	Sol
4	Fa
3	Mi
2	Re
1	Do

In the following song, the words have been omitted and tonic sol-fa syllables substituted for the first line. Write in the correct syllables before proceeding with the rest of the page.

Do re mi do, do re mi do, mi fa sol, mi fa sol,

If you have trouble determining the syllable names for the second line of the song, number the notes according to their scale degrees, then substitute the syllables from the chart at the top of the page.

Turn to the next frame.

282

Diagnostic Question Six

Tonic sol-fa syllables have been written below the notes of three musical excerpts on the right. Which one of the three excerpts correctly identifies all of the notes?

Alternatives

		frame
a.	I am unsure of the answer.	281
b.	Number 1 is correct.	285
c.	Number 2 is correct.	287
d.	Number 3 is correct.	296

283

That was not correct. Please read the explanation in frame 292.

284

Naturally. By being careful, it is easy to determine the I, IV, and V chords. Here are a few more examples for practice, but remember:

$$\begin{aligned} \text{I} &= \text{tonic} \\ \text{IV} &= \text{subdominant} \\ \text{V} &= \text{dominant} \end{aligned}$$

Use the Shield.

In A major, the tonic chord consists of which notes?

🕊

A, C-sharp, E *(Watch the sharps!)*

In B-flat major, the notes of the dominant chord are _____, _____, _____.

🕊

F, A, C *(Count up five notes from B-flat, then add the next two spaces. B♭ counts as note 1.)*

In D major, the subdominant chord is made up of _____, _____, _____.

🕊

G, B, D *(Count up four notes from D, then add the next two lines.)*

In C major, the dominant chord has _____, _____, and _____.

🕊

G, B, D *(Count up five notes from C, then add the next two lines.)*

Please turn to frame 294.

285

No, some of the notes in that excerpt were incorrectly identified. Here is the process that you need to follow.

1. Determine the key of the music. In this case the key signature is one sharp (F#), so the key is G major.
2. Locate the "home tone" of the key (the note G) and assign it the syllable "do."
3. Working from that note, number all the other notes in the passage with numbers 1 to 8. Then convert the numbers to syllables. (If you need help with the conversion to syllables, consult the chart in frame 281.)

Now return to frame 282 and answer the question.

286

Return to frame 303.

That's right. Now use the shield and answer the following questions.

Use the Shield.

The first and eighth tones of the scale are both called (_____) in this system.

do

The fifth tone of the scale is _____ and resolves either direction to *do* (both 1 and 8 are *do*).

sol

In the C-major scale, the note E has the sol-fa name _____.

mi

In the G-major scale, the note E has the sol-fa name _____.

la

So far we have identified the notes of the scale with numbers (1–8) and syllables (sol-fa). Each note of the scale also has a name that is frequently used to identify the chord or triad built on that tone. All of the names are identified below for the C-major scale.

The names of the I, IV, and V chords are important to you and should be learned. They will be required later in the program.

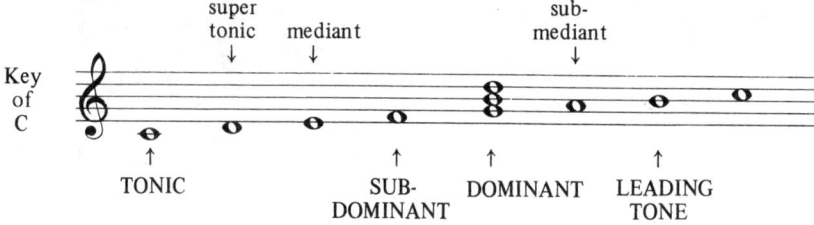

Continued on the next page.

Any triad built on a scale tone will carry the same name as that tone. On the previous page, a chord has been constructed on G, the *dominant tone* of the C major scale. The chord is therefore known as the dominant chord or triad. *It is imperative to remember that the chord names for particular notes change when keys change.* For instance, the chord built on G in the example above is the *dominant chord* in the key of C. In the key of G (see for example below) it is the *tonic chord.* Although the two chords possess exactly the same notes, they serve different functions in their respective keys.

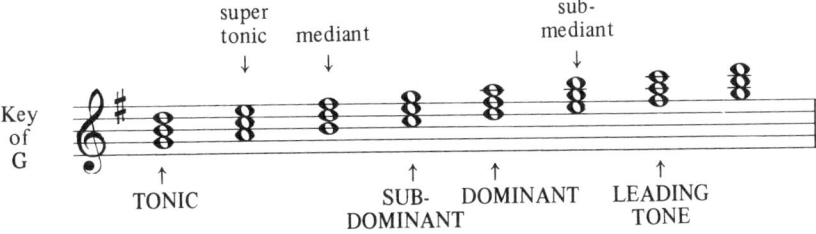

The three chords identified with capital letters in the example above (the tonic or I chord, the subdominant or IV chord, and the dominant or V chord) have an important characteristic in common. If you examine each of the chords in the example to determine their quality, you will discover that only the chords I, IV, and V are major triads. That is always the case. *The I, IV, and V chords are naturally major in all major keys.* They are known as the **primary** chords of the key.

The *tonic chord* is the fundamental chord of the key—the "home" chord, where resolution is achieved in most music. The *dominant chord* consists of tones 5, 7 and 2, all of which resolve to 1. The resulting chord is, therefore, dominant in its tendency to resolve to the tonic. The *subdominant chord* is not as important as the dominant and tonic chords, but because of its major quality and its use in traditional Western music it can be considered the third most important chord in any given key. The importance of knowing these three chords in several keys cannot be overemphasized. They are the basis of many songs, and may be used to accompany them.

Turn to the next frame.

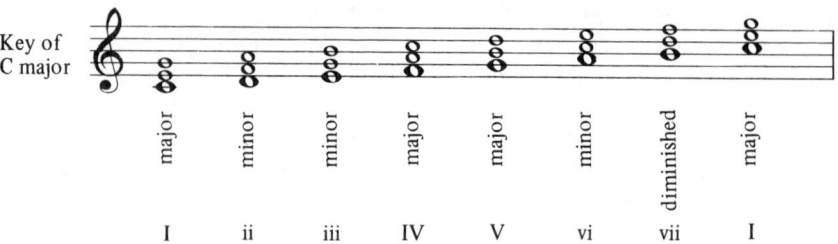

Do you notice that the last chord is the same as chord 1? It is merely one octave higher. The *primary* chords are designated by the upper-case roman numerals I, IV, and V to indicate that they are major chords. The chords of secondary importance are 2, 3, and 6. These chords are designated with lower-case roman numerals to indicate their minor nature as follows: ii iii, vi. (The vii chord has special characteristics that will not be discussed here.)

Use the Shield.

If you form a major scale on any note, will the triads on notes 1, 4, and 5 of the scale always be major?

Certainly. The I, IV, and V chords of all major keys are major.

On the staff directly below, which chords are major?

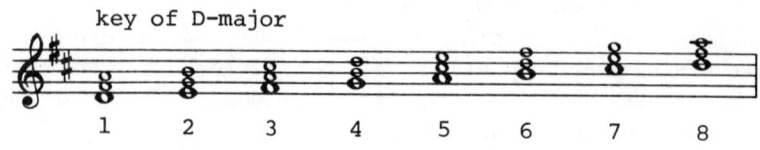

Chords 1, 4, and 5, i.e., the chords on notes D, G, and A are major in the D-major scale. (Don't forget the sharps.)

Which chords are major in this scale?

Turn to frame 290 for the answer

290

The chords on notes F, B♭, and C are major. They are found on notes 1, 4, and 5 of the F-major scale. (Remember, the B on note 4 is B♭, as indicated by the flat in the key signature.)

Now continue with the Diagnostic Question.

Diagnostic Question Seven

From the alternatives below, choose the one that correctly identifies the I, IV, and V chords in the key of A major.

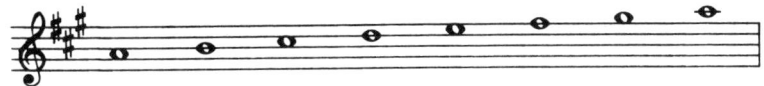

Alternatives

		frame
a.	I would like to see the review first.	292
b.	I chord = A, C, E IV chord = D, F, A V chord = E, G, B	283
c.	I chord = A, C♯, E IV chord = D, F♯, A V chord = E, G♯, B	284
d.	I chord = A, C♯, E IV chord = D♯, F, A V chord = E, G, B♯	293

291

No, you have matched the wrong items. For pertinent information, go to frame 295.

Here is how to identify the notes in the I, IV, and V chords of any given key.

Let's take the key of E-flat major as an example. It has three flats: B-flat, E-flat, and A-flat. The key tone is, of course, E-flat. By writing the tones of that scale on the staff below, we can begin our analysis.

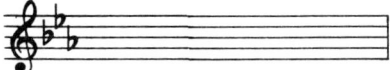

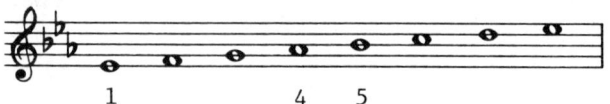

The next step is to mark notes 1, 4, and 5, thereby identifying the notes on which the tonic, subdominant, and dominant chords will be built.

The notes in any triad fall on consecutive lines or spaces, whichever the case may be. As seen above, the I chord begins on the bottom line (E-flat). It will, therefore, include the next two lines (G and B-flat). The IV chord begins on the second space up (A-flat), and includes the next two spaces (C and E-flat). The V chord begins on the third line from the bottom (B-flat) and includes the next two lines (D and F).

Briefly, here are the steps just used:

1. Identify the key signature and put it on the staff.

2. Write in the notes of the scale and identify notes 1, 4, and 5.

3. Determine the notes of each triad by identifying the two consecutive lines or spaces above the first, fourth, and fifth notes.

Use the Shield.

What are the notes of the I chord and V chord in B-flat major?

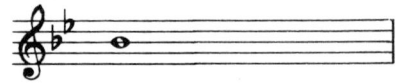

$I = B\flat, D, F; V = F, A, C.$ The I chord starts on the key tone (B-flat), as shown on the right. The V chord starts five notes higher, on F.

Go back to frame 290 and answer the Diagnostic Question.

293

That was not the correct alternative. Please go to frame 292.

294

Diagnostic Question Eight

In the three columns below, the name, number, and characteristics of three chords are given. Match the items in the three columns and choose the correct alternative from those at the bottom of the page. (Your answer will be something like A-2-X.)

A. dominant	1. IV chord	X. This chord is based on the key tone. It is the fundamental chord of any key.
B. tonic	2. V chord	Y. This chord is the most used chord for departure from the home chord. It is second to the home chord in importance.
C. subdominant	3. I chord	Z. This is one of the three major chords in a major key. Although widely used, it is not as important to the key as the chord described in Y above.

Alternatives

		frame
a.	Please provide an explanation.	295
b.	A-2-X; B-3-Z; C-1-Y	297
c.	A-2-Y; B-3-Z; C-1-X	291
d.	A-2-Y; B-3-X; C-1-Z	298

295

Here is the explanation.

The tonic chord (I) is the fundamental chord of the key and is built on the first note of the scale. Toward this chord, most music "strives"; when it is reached, a feeling of conclusion or finality is achieved. The tonic chord, therefore, has been identified as the *home* chord.

The dominant chord (V) is the second strongest chord in any key. When composers want to progress from the tonic chord to another chord, they usually progress through the dominant chord, even if they go through several other chords on the way. It is the most common chord of departure from the tonic.

The subdominant chord (IV) is the third of the three major chords in any major key. Its quality ranks it among the three strongest chords, but it holds a less important position than the I and V chords.

To summarize:

I is the tonic, the strongest chord in the key; built on the key tone; a chord of conclusion.

IV is the subdominant, the third strongest chord in the key; built on the fourth tone of the scale; a secondary chord of departure from I.

V is the dominant, the second strongest chord in the key; built on the fifth tone of the scale; primary chord of departure from I.

Return to the Diagnostic Question in frame 294 and see if you can now answer it correctly.

296

There was a mistake in that alternative. Go to frame 285 for an explanation.

297

No, you have matched the wrong items. For an explanation, turn to frame 295.

298

Certainly. The chords match as follows:

Tonic, the I chord. This chord includes the key tone and is the fundamental chord of any key.

Dominant, the V chord. This chord is the one most used for departure from the tonic chord. It is second to the tonic chord in importance.

Subdominant, the IV chord. This is one of the three major chords in any major key. Although widely used, it is not as important to the key as the dominant chord.

Thus far, we have not discussed the chords on the other tones of the major scale except to say that three are minor and are therefore designated with lower-case numerals.

Although the following generalization is deceptive because it is not always true, it is worth mentioning. Each of the three major chords (I, IV, and V) has a minor substitute as follows:

$$\begin{array}{rccc} \text{chord:} & \text{I} & \text{IV} & \text{V} \\ \text{substitute:} & \text{vi} & \text{ii} & \text{iii (or vii)} \end{array}$$

The minor chords may occasionally be substituted for the related major chords with pleasant results. Notice that the root tone of each substitute chord is located a minor third below the root tone of the major chord. The substitutes are, therefore, termed *relative minor chords*. Minor scales built on their root tones are *relative minor scales*, which will be discussed in Chapter 6.

Now go to frame 299.

Use the Shield.

A substitute for the I chord could be the _____ chord.

🦢

vi (down 2 steps from 1 or 8)

A substitute for the IV chord could be the _____ chord.

🦢

ii (down 2 steps from 4)

A substitute for the V chord could be the _____ chord.

🦢

iii

The relative minor of the I chord is the _____ chord.

🦢

vi

The relative minor of the V chord is the _____ chord.

🦢

iii

The relative minor of the IV chord is the _____ chord.

🦢

ii

Turn to frame 300.

The V chord has one other characteristic that deserves attention. It is frequently referred to as the V_7 (five-seven) chord when the *tone on the seventh step* of that chord is added. See the following example in the key of C major.

From the root tone of this chord (G), the new tone is seven steps away. When the new tone is added, the chord is known as a V_7 or *dominant-seventh* chord. The new tone is always added on the next consecutive line or space. Its addition increases the chord's "feeling of restlessness" and its demand for resolution to the tonic chord.

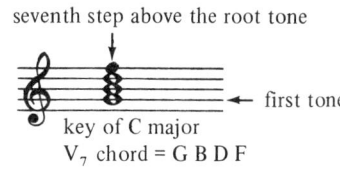

A dominant seventh (V_7) chord is merely a V chord plus _____.

Check your answer in frame 301.

ANSWER: The seventh tone *of that chord*.

Congratulations, you have now completed Chapter 5 of the program. The following Skill Builders will help you develop skills relating to the concepts just learned. Do each of the suggested activities until you feel comfortable with the process.

Skill Builders

1. Sing the song "A Frog Went A-Courting," first using words, then sol-fa syllables, and finally tone numbers for the scale degree represented by each note. You may have to sing the song at a slower tempo in order to do it right the first few times. Then sing other songs in the book using the same process.

Turn to the next frame.

302

A FROG WENT A-COURTING

English Folk Song

Verse 2. He rode up to Miss Mousie's door, uh-huh
He rode up to Miss Mousie's door, uh-huh
He rode up to Miss Mousie's door
With his coat all buttoned down before, uh-huh, uh-huh, uh-huh.

Verse 3. He took Miss Mousie on his knee, uh-huh
He took Miss Mousie on his knee, uh-huh
He took Miss Mousie on his knee
And said "My dear, will you marry me?" uh-huh, uh-huh, uh-huh.

Continued in the next frame.

Verse 4.   Oh no, kind sir, I can't do that, huh-uh
             Oh no, kind sir, I can't do that, huh-uh
             Oh no, kind sir, I can't do that
             You'll have to ask my Uncle Rat, huh-uh, huh-uh, huh-uh.

Verse 5.   Then Uncle Rat gave his consent, uh-huh, uh-huh
             Then Uncle Rat gave his consent, uh-huh, uh-huh
             Then Uncle Rat gave his consent, so they got married
             And off they went, uh-huh, uh-huh, uh-huh.

2. Play "A Frog Went A-Courting" on the piano (with one hand or two), or on some other instrument until you can play it without interruption.

3. "The Muffin Man" is written below in the key of G. On the blank staff lines at the top of frame 304, transpose the song to the key of F major. To transpose, think of each note, not by note name, but by its sol-fa syllable or by its assigned number, 1–8, in the scale. Then write the note in the key of F bearing the same syllable or number. Do not neglect the F major key signature. When finished, check your work in frame 286.

MUFFIN MAN

Verse 2.   Oh, yes I know the Muffin Man. . . .
Verse 3.   Have you see the Muffin Man? . . .
Verse 4.   Oh, yes I've seen the Muffin Man. . . .
Verse 5.   Do you like the Muffin Man? . . .
Verse 6.   Oh, yes I like the Muffin Man. . . .

Turn to frame 304.

4. Identify by name the chords used to harmonize the song, "Michael Finnigin" and write the appropriate chord name above each measure.

MICHAEL FINNIGIN

Anonymous
Folk Song

1. There was a man named Michael Finnigin,
He had whiskers on his chin-i-gin, Wind blew 'em off, but they grew in a-gin, Poor old Michael Finnigin!

Verses 2 and 3 are found in the next frame.

Verse 2. There was a man named Michael Finnigin.
He went fishing with a pin agin,
Caught a fish but dropped it in agin,
Poor old Michael Finnigin.

Verse 3. There was a man named Michael Finnigin,
Climbed a tree and barked his shin agin,
Took off several years of skin agin,
Poor old Michael Finnigin.

5. Sing the round *Are You Sleeping?* Then sing the Hawaiian version of it found below.

LILI OU KALANI

Li - li ou ka - la - ni, Li - li ou ka - la - ni,
Pe hea oe, Pe hea oe, Mai kai no,
mai kai no, fish and poi, fish and poi.

Turn to the next page for the Self-Test.

306

Self-Test

You are now ready to evaluate your understanding of the material in this chapter so you can determine which concepts you should review.

Listed below are five terms and five definitions. Write the letter of the correct definition by each term.

1. key ____

2. tonality ____

3. key tone ____

4. scale ____

A. a series of tones in ascending or descending order, beginning with the key tone, and maintaining fixed distances between all tones

B. any group of tones that are drawn to a central tone, *and bear its name*

C. the organization of tones around a key tone—the tendency to return to a key tone for the feeling of conclusion

D. the central tone to which other tones are drawn—where complete repose is found

Shown below is an example of the G-major scale. Under certain notes are numbers and blanks. Use each blank to write the number of the note directly above it, indicating the note's position in relation to the rest of the notes in the scale.

5.____   6.____   7.____ 8.____

9. ____ In any major scale, the notes are all whole steps apart except for two places, where the notes are only half steps apart. Write the numbers of the notes
10. ____ between which the half steps exist in blanks 9 and 10.

Turn to frame 307.

11. A scale is represented below by the numbers 1 through 8. Draw an arrow from note 7 to its note of resolution. Then do the same for notes 2 and 5.

    1 2 3 4 5 6 7 8

12. Are any chords employed in "A Frog Went A-Courting" not primary triads? If so, what chords are they, and where are they located? _____
    _____

In the tonic sol-fa system each note of the scale has a syllable. Write the correct syllable under each specified note of the A-major scale below.

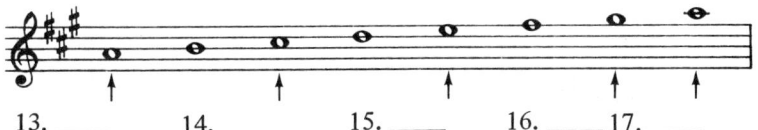

13. ____   14. ____   15. ____   16. ____ 17. ____

Identify each of the following key signatures.

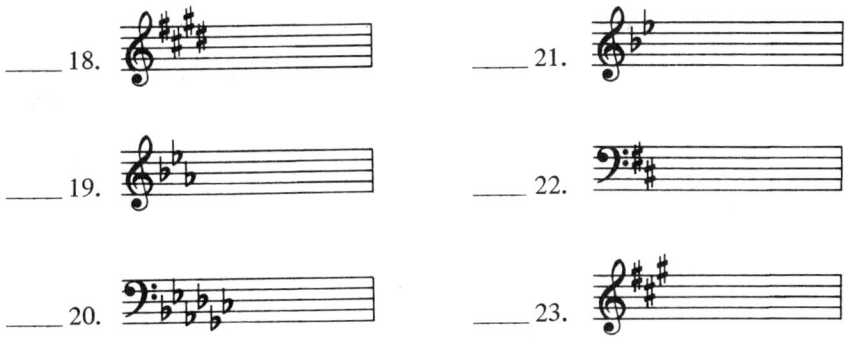

____ 18.   ____ 21.

____ 19.   ____ 22.

____ 20.   ____ 23.

Go to frame 308.

24. _____ to _____   In the key of A major, the half steps fall between which notes?
25. _____ to _____   (Write your answers in numbers 24 and 25.)

26. _____ to _____   Where will they fall in the key of B-flat major? (Write your answers
27. _____ to _____   in blanks 26 and 27.)

On the staff below is the B-flat major scale with chords built on each scale tone. Each of these chords has a name. Write the chord name under the chords that are indicated.

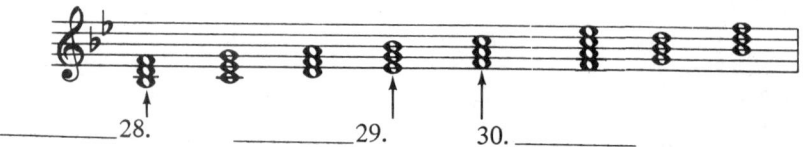

_____ 28.   _____ 29.   30. _____

Match the next three items correctly and write your answer in the blank at the left.

31. tonic chord _____   A. the second most important chord in the key—the primary chord of departure

32. subdominant chord _____   B. the fundamental chord of any key, toward which all other chords in the key lead

33. dominant chord _____   C. the third most important chord in any key

34. _____ Which chord may be substituted for the I chord?

35. _____ For the IV chord?

36. _____ For the V chord?

37. _____ In the example at the right is the V chord in the key of A major. To make it a V_7 chord what note would you add?

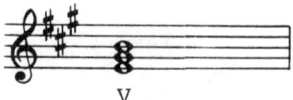

Turn to frame 309.

Determine the names of the following three mystery tunes by translating the sol-fa system into real pitches. The rhythm is not precisely notated, but the measures are marked with slashes, and arrows indicate whether to move up or down from the preceding pitch.

38. sol↓ mi↑ sol–/ sol mi sol–/ la sol fa mi/ re mi fa mi fa/sol↓ do do do/ do re mi fa sol

    ANSWER: _____

39. sol la sol fa/ mi fa sol–/ re mi fa–/ mi fa sol–/ sol la sol fa/ mi fa sol–/ re–sol–/ mi do

    ANSWER: _____

40. sol/↑ do do do do/ do–re/ mi mi mi mi/ mi–/↑ sol–sol la/ sol↓ mi do re/ mi mi re re/ do–

    ANSWER: _____

41. In the blank space below, complete these 7 steps:
    a. Draw the five lines of the staff across the entire page.
    b. Put the bass clef sign on the staff.
    c. Write in the key signature for B♭ major.
    d. Write in the notes of the B♭-major scale on the staff.
    e. Write in the notes of the I, IV, and V chords.
    f. Make a V_7 chord out of the V chord by adding the appropriate note.
    g. Write the names of the chords under notes 1, 4, and 5.

End of test.

Please check your answers with those in the key that follows. Be sure to review each missed question by looking up the topic in parenthesis. If you missed a substantial number of the questions you should review the entire chapter before going on.

Answers & Review Index

1. B (key defined, 249)
2. C (tonality defined, 249)
3. D (key tone defined, 249)
4. A (scale defined, 249)
5. 2 (scale tone numbers, 252)
6. 4 (scale tone numbers, 252)
7. 7 (scale tone numbers, 252)
8. 8 or 1 (scale tone numbers, 252)
9. 3–4 (major scale half steps, 260)
10. 7–8 (major scale half steps, 260)
11. 1 2 3 4 5 6 7 8 (resolution of scale tones, 255)
12. No, they are all primary chords; I, IV, V (primary chords, 298)
13. do (tonic sol-fa system, 281)
14. mi (tonic sol-fa system, 281)
15. sol (tonic sol-fa system, 281)
16. ti (tonic sol-fa system, 281)
17. do (tonic sol-fa system, 281)
18. E major (key signatures, 274 ff)
19. E-flat major (key signatures, 274 ff)
20. G-flat major (key signatures, 274 ff)
21. B-flat major (key signatures, 274 ff)
22. D major (key signatures, 274 ff)
23. A major (key signatures, 274 ff)
24. C-sharp-D (major scale half steps, 260)
25. G-sharp-A (major scale half steps, 260)
26. D-E-flat (major scale half steps, 260)
27. A-B-flat (major scale half steps, 260)
28. tonic (chord names, 295)
29. subdominant (chord names, 295)
30. dominant (chord names, 295)
31. B (tonic chord, 295)
32. C (subdominant chord, 295)
33. A (dominant chord, 295)
34. vi (substitute for I chord, 298)
35. ii (substitute for IV chord, 298)
36. iii (substitute for V chord, 298)

Continued from the previous page.

37. D (V_7 chord, 300)
38. "This Old Man" (tonic sol-fa system, 281)
39. "London Bridge" (tonic sol-fa system, 281)
40. "Farmer in the Dell" system, 281)
41.

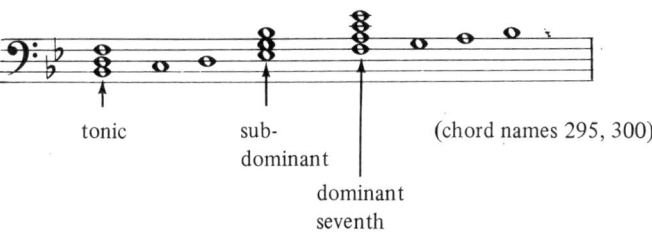

tonic   sub-dominant   dominant seventh   (chord names 295, 300)

Chapter 6 begins in the next frame.

6
Minor Scales, Chords, and Keys

311

Although much of the material in the previous chapter pertains to minor, as well as major, scales and keys, there has been no discussion of minor keys and scales as such. The minor keys do much to enhance the sounds of music by bringing another dimension to the listener's ear. Whereas there is only one kind of major scale, there are three kinds of minor scales. The emphasis in this chapter will be on identifying minor keys, scales, and chords, and their unique characteristics.

Objectives

1. Locate the relative minor scale for any major scale, and specify its key signature.
2. Recall two ways major scales are like their relative minor scales, and two ways they are different.
3. Differentiate between a *natural* minor scale and a *harmonic* minor scale visually and verbally.
4. Recall the construction of minor triads, and how they differ from major triads.
5. Employ the minor circle of fifths to ascertain minor key signatures.
6. Identify the tones and the primary chords of the natural minor keys of C, A, and D.
7. Identify the tones and primary chords of the harmonic minor keys of C, A, and D.
8. Learn the note names of the minor scale in the tonic sol-fa system, and identify its relation to the system in major keys.

In this chapter there are six Diagnostic Questions. Now turn to the next frame.

In the last chapter the I, IV, and V chords were introduced as the primary chords of the major scale. Then substitute chords were shown for each of the three.

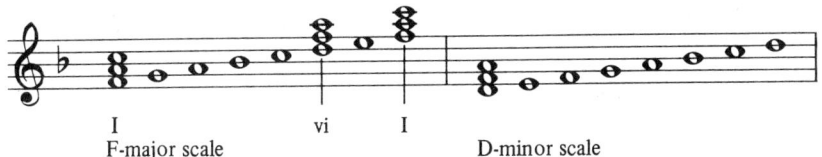

I   vi   I
F-major scale   D-minor scale

The substitute for the I chord was the vi chord. In the F-major scale above, the vi chord is based on the note D, *which is located a minor third below F.* If you construct a scale on that note, the resulting scale will be the relative minor scale of F major, namely, D minor.

Diagnostic Question One

What scale is the relative minor scale for G major?

Alternatives

		frame
a.	I'm not sure. Please review it for me.	313
b.	C minor	314
c.	D minor	316
d.	E minor	318

Here is a review. Every major scale has a relative minor scale. The relative minor scale can be found by establishing the home tone of the major scale in your mind, and then determining what note falls a minor third below. The scale based on this new note is always the relative minor scale of the original major scale.

1. The C major scale is shown on the right. It's home tone is C.

2. The note found a third below C is the note A.

3. Because A is only 1½ steps below C it is a *minor* third below. (See frame 218 if a review is needed.)

4. The scale built on that note is the A-minor scale. It is the relative minor scale of C major.

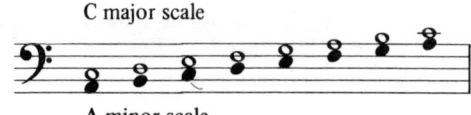

C major scale

A minor scale

Now return to frame 312 and answer the question.

314

Not quite. An explanation is found in frame 313.

315

It may seem confusing now, but it will become easy to locate relative minor keys. Assume, for example, that we have a major scale beginning on the note E♭. The rule quoted earlier said that the relative minor scale always begins on the note a *minor third lower*.

1. If we are working with the key of E♭ major, we must find the note a *third* lower, in this example, middle C.

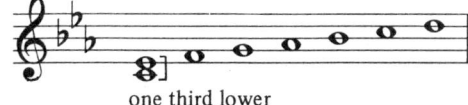
one third lower

2. Determine whether the third is of major or minor quality. From E♭ to C comprises 1½ steps (not 2) so it is a minor third.

3. Having found the note a minor third below, we know the scale built on it is the relative minor of E♭ major. In this case, the key of C minor.

Now try this example: What is the relative minor scale of F major? (Use the staff below to figure out your answer.)

1. What note is a third lower than F?
2. Is that third of major or minor quality?

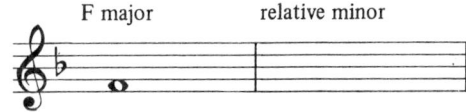
F major   relative minor

3. If it is a minor third, the scale beginning on that note is the relative minor scale. If it is a major third, raise your bottom note one half step so it becomes a minor third, and *that note* is the relative minor.

Now turn to the Diagnostic Question in frame 319 and apply the rule. (By the way, the answer to the above question is D minor.)

316

Not quite. An explanation is found in frame 313.

Correct. You have picked the relative minor scale for each of three major scales.

As you noticed in the objectives for this chapter, there are several kinds of minor scales. You have been dealing with the *natural minor scale*. It exists naturally a minor third below its relative major scale, and uses the same key signature.

Let's examine the natural minor scale of C to discover some of its characteristics.

QUESTION: What is the key signature for the key of C minor?

ANSWER: Three flats: B♭, E♭, A♭. (The same as its relative major scale, E♭ major.)

Here are the C-major and C-minor scales. What differences do you see?

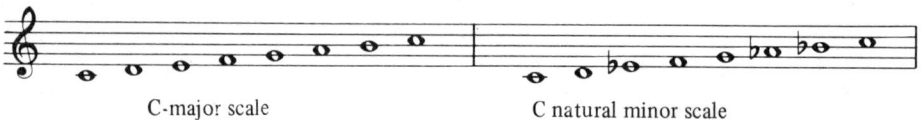

C-major scale   C natural minor scale

Differences

1. Compared with the C-major scale, the C-minor scale has lowered steps 3, 6, and 7.
2. The half steps fall between 2-3 and 5-6 in the minor scale, a change from the major scale.

If you compare other major scales and minor scales, these differences will exist.

Use the Shield.

When comparing major scales with natural minor scales, what notes are changed, and how?

Notes 3, 6, and 7 are lowered one half step.

The notes of the G-major scale are G A B C D E F♯ G. What are the notes of the G-minor scale?

G A B♭ C D E♭ F♮ G   *(notes 3, 6, 7 have been lowered)*

Turn to frame 321.

You're right. Let's analyze these two scales and see what similarities and differences exist.

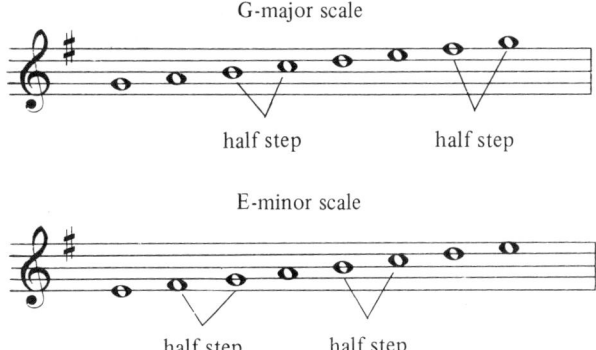

Similarities

1. They have the same key signature: one sharp. When a major and minor scale have the same key signature they are called *relative* keys.
2. They both have notes on every line and space—no gaps.

Differences

1. They start on different notes. Very important: *The relative minor scale starts a minor third lower than the major scale.* Thus, in the example above, the G-major scale begins on G, and its relative minor scale on E.
2. The half steps do not occur in the same places.
   In the major scale: half steps between notes 3—4 and 7—8.
   In the minor scale: half steps between notes 2—3 and 6—7.
   As you can see, the half steps occur one note lower in the minor scale.

Remember, every major scale has a relative minor scale that uses the same key signature, and begins a minor third lower.

Now turn to frame 319.

319

Diagnostic Question Two

On the left are names of three major scales. On the right are three minor scales. Choose the *relative minor scale* for each of the major scales.

Major Scales	Minor Scales
F major	A minor
C major	G minor
B♭ major	D minor

Alternatives

		frame
a.	I'm not sure. Please explain how to find relative keys.	315
b.	F major and D minor C major and A minor B♭ major and G minor	317
c.	F major and A minor C major and G minor B♭ major and D minor	323
d.	F major and G minor C major and D minor B♭ major and A minor	326

320

That wasn't quite right. Please read the information in frame 322.

321

Use the Shield.

The notes of the F-major scale are F G A B♭ C D E F. What are the notes of the F natural minor scale?

F G A♭ B♭ C D♭ E♭ F   *(Notes 3, 6, 7 have been lowered.)*

The notes of the A-major scale are A B C♯ D E F♯ G♯ A. What are the notes of the A natural minor scale?

A B C D E F G A   *(Lowering notes 3, 6, 7 cancels the sharps.)*

What is the relative minor scale for A♭ major?

F minor   (a minor third lower)

What is the key signature for A minor?

The same as its relative major, C major: no sharps or flats.

What natural minor scale has the same key signature as F major?

D minor   (one flat: B♭)

Go to frame 325.

322

The primary chords in major keys are major chords, designated by the roman numerals I, IV, and V. In the natural minor scale, the primary chords *all become minor chords*, designated by the roman numerals i, iv, and v. Turn to frame 327.

That was an incorrect alternative. Please read the information in frame 315.

That is right. The primary chords in the natural minor scale are all minor chords, designated by roman numerals i, iv, an v. The reason is easy to see. On the top staff below is the D-major scale; the black notes will be lowered to create the minor scale. On the bottom staff is the D-minor scale, with the primary triads constructed on notes 1, 4, and 5. Notice that the middle note in each triad is lowered, making the bottom third minor and thereby changing that triad from major to minor.

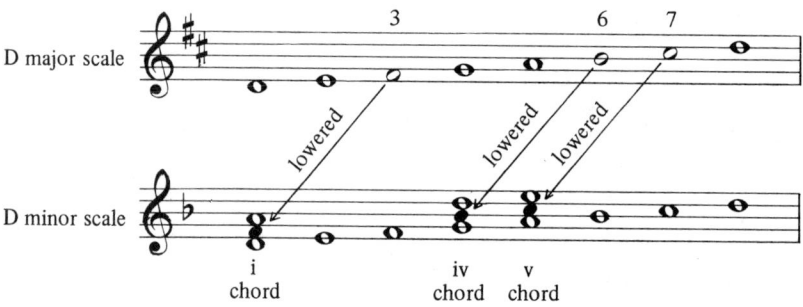

NOTE: Those three notes were lowered automatically when the major key signature of two sharps was changed to the minor key signature of one flat.

Go to frame 332.

325

The key signatures for minor scales can also be determined by using a circle of fifths. Comparison of this circle of fifths to the circle in frame 274 will show the differences between major and minor key signatures.

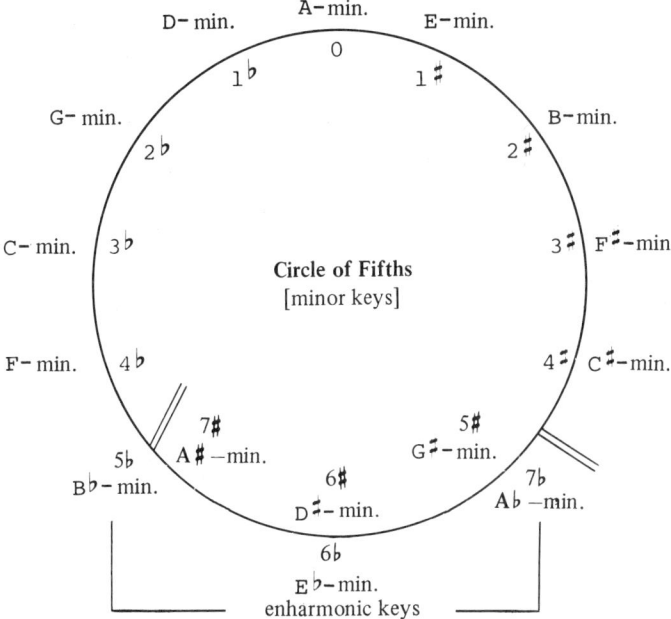

Circle of Fifths [minor keys]

SUPPORTIVE SKILL: In any key signature using sharps, the sharps always appear in the same order as for major scales, namely, F♯, C♯, G♯, D♯, A♯, E♯, B♯. In any key signature involving flats, the flats always appear in the same order: B♭, E♭, A♭, D♭, G♭, C♭, F♭. Whatever number of sharps or flats a key signature uses, they will be in the order listed above.

Go on to frame 327.

326

That wasn't quite right. Please read the information in frame 315.

===== 327 =====

Diagnostic Question Three

The primary chords in any key are the I, IV, and V chords. What happens to these chords in the natural minor scale?

Alternatives

		frame
a.	I'm not sure, and I don't want to guess.	322
b.	The primary chords remain major chords in the natural minor scale.	320
c.	The primary chords all become minor chords in the natural minor scale.	324
d.	The primary chords cease to exist as primary chords in the natural minor scale.	331

===== 328 =====

I'm sorry. That was not the correct alternative. Please turn to frame 329.

The explanation is very simple. There is only one difference between natural minor and harmonic minor scales:

A natural minor scale can be converted to a harmonic minor scale by raising its seventh tone by one half step.

By raising the seventh tone of the scale by one half step it is back to the same position as the seventh tone of the major scale. In this position it is called the leading tone because it pulls so strongly up to "do." Musicians like the color of the minor scale, but do not want to lose the tendencies of the leading tone in their harmonies. As a compromise they preserved the lowered third and sixth steps of the natural minor scale, but raised the seventh tone back to its earlier position and named the scale the *harmonic minor*. Turn to frame 332 and answer the question.

That wasn't correct. Please go to frame 338 for an explanation.

331

That wasn't quite right. Please read the information in frame 322.

332

We have explored the natural minor scale and several of its characteristics. To review:

1. Its key signature is the same as its relative major, which is found a minor third above.
2. Its primary triads are all minor.
3. It is different from major scales in that its half steps are now found between steps 2–3 and 5–6. This fact changes the tone tendencies with the scale and gives its melodies and harmonies their distinctive flavor.

It is now time to examine another minor scale, the *harmonic minor*.

Diagnostic Question Four

How does the *harmonic* minor scale differ from the *natural* minor scale?

Alternatives

		frame
a.	I don't know. How about an explanation?	329
b.	The third, sixth, and seventh steps of the natural minor are lowered to create the harmonic minor.	328
c.	The harmonic minor begins on the note found a minor third below the first note of the natural minor scale.	334
d.	The seventh step of the natural minor is raised to make the harmonic minor.	335

Absolutely right. You seem to understand the construction of chords in the harmonic minor. Do these next few exercises.

C-minor scale (harmonic minor)

Use the Shield.

In the above example (key of C minor), the i chord will consist of which notes?

C, E-flat, and G   *(Be sure to watch for the flats.)*

In the same example, the iv chord will consist of which notes?

F, A-flat, and C

The V chord will consist of which notes?

G, B, and D (Remember the leading tone of the harmonic minor is only one half step from the tonic. This explains the B natural above, and the major quality of the V chord.)

The C minor scale is the relative minor of what major scale?

E♭ major (Both key signatures have 3 flats: B♭, E♭, A♭.)

There is only one difference between the C natural minor scale and the C harmonic minor scale. What is the difference?

The B♭ of the natural minor is raised to a B♮ in the harmonic minor.

Turn to frame 341.

I'm sorry. That was not the correct alternative. Please turn to frame 329.

You are right. The harmonic minor differs from the natural minor in one simple way: *The seventh step is raised one half step.*

That's a simple change, but it involves several interesting ramifications:

1. The reason the seventh step is raised is to keep it one half step away from *do*, thus preserving its strong tendencies as the leading tone to *do*. The distance between the seventh and eighth steps (one half step) is the same as it is in the major scale.

2. This change in the seventh step **does not** take place in the key signature. It is raised on the staff every time it appears by adding the proper *accidental* (a sharp, a flat, or a natural sign).

3. In the natural minor scale, the primary triads are all minor. When the seventh step is raised in the harmonic minor, the resulting V chord is *major*.

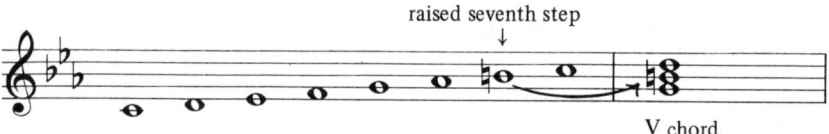

The principal triads of the harmonic minor scale are i (minor triad), iv (minor triad), and V (major triad).

Turn to frame 336.

336

Diagnostic Question Five

Carefully select the correct response below.

Which of the following alternatives correctly identifies the i, iv, and V chords in the key of A harmonic minor?

Alternatives

		frame
a.	I don't quite understand. Please direct me to an explanation.	338
b.	i chord = A C E iv chord = D F A V chord = E G B	330
c.	i chord = A C♯ E iv chord = D F♯ A V chord = E G♯ B	340
d.	i chord = A C E iv chord = D F A V chord = E G♯ B	333

337

Here are the correct sol-fa syllables for the last line of *Heigh-ho, Nobody's Home*. Check them with your work in frame 342. Then continue with the program on that page.

338

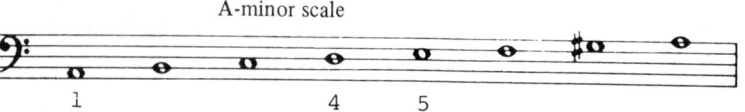

A-minor scale

In the question you were asked to identify the notes of the i, iv, and V chords in A minor. In the example above, notes 1, 4, and 5, which will form the respective roots of the three triads, are identified.

Triads

- i = Note A and the two spaces above A, namely, C and E.
- iv = Note D and the two lines above D, namely, F and A.
- V = Note E and the two spaces above E, namely, G and B. (The G is sharped because it is the seventh step of the harmonic minor scale.)

> i is a minor triad.
> iv is a minor triad.
> V is a major triad.

Return to frame 336.

339

That is correct. You have identified the syllables for a musical excerpt in the minor key. This completes the Diagnostic Questions for Chapter 6. Turn to frame 344 for THE NEXT STEP . . . and the Skill Builders which follow.

Well, you seem to be confused about something. The review that will help you is in frame 338.

In Chapter 5, the tonic sol-fa system was presented for the major scale as shown on the left below.

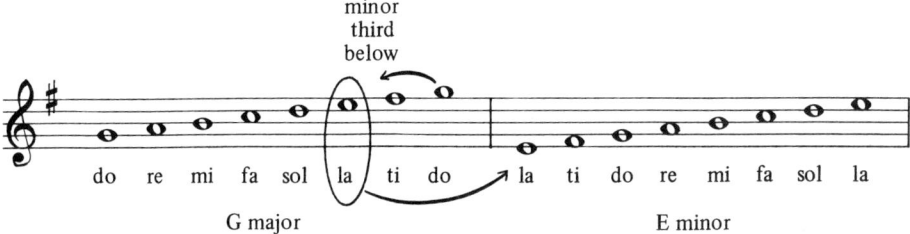

Just as the natural minor scale begins a minor third lower than its relative major, the tonic sol-fa system for minor scales begins a minor third lower, on *la*. (Compare the two scales above.) All half steps are thereby brought to their correct places, and the home tone acquires a new name, *la*.

In the song, *Heigh-ho, Nobody's Home*, on the following page, the sol-fa syllables have been written under the first line of music. Write the syllables under the second line, check your answers, and then proceed with the program.

Turn to the next frame.

342

HEIGH-HO, NOBODY'S HOME

(You can check your answer in frame 337.)

Use the Shield.

In the key of C minor, what syllable designates note 1 in the example at the right?

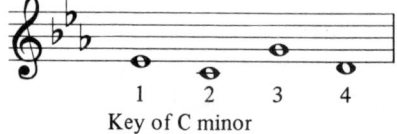

do (It is the third note in that minor scale; la, ti, do.)

What syllable designates note 2?

la (It is the home tone.)

What syllable designates note 3?

mi

What syllable designates note 4?

ti

Diagnostic Question Six is in frame 343.

343

Diagnostic Question Six

Which of the following musical passages is *correctly* labeled in the tonic sol-fa system?

Alternatives

		frame
a.	I need to reread the explanation of tonic sol-fa before I answer.	341
b.	Key of C minor	345
c.	Key of G minor	339
d.	Key of A minor	346

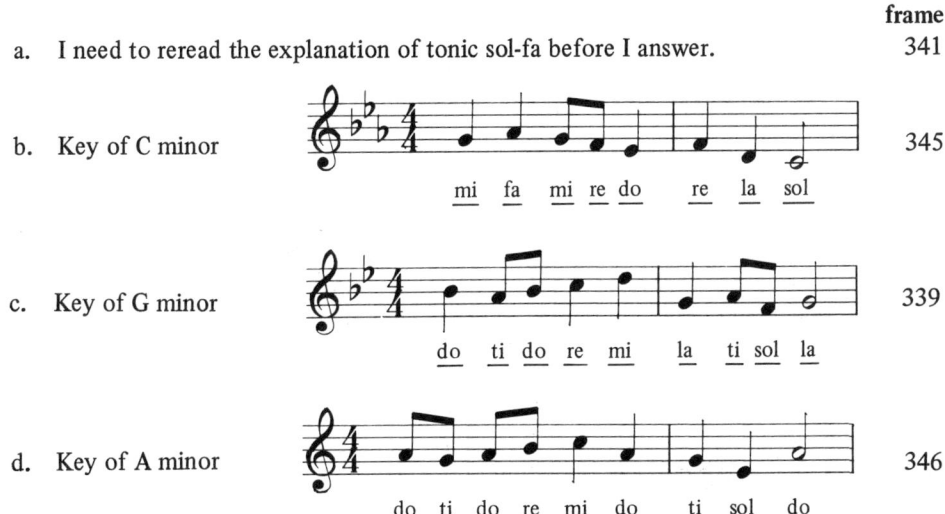

344

♦ THE NEXT STEP...

There is one other minor scale that you may want to be familiar with. It is known as the *melodic minor*, and it follows the normal tendencies of melodies to move up (toward the tonic) in one way, and move down (toward the dominant) in another way. It therefore uses one set of notes if the melody is ascending, and a different set if the melody descends. The descending scale is easy to remember. It is the natural minor scale, the first one we explored in the chapter, and it follows the minor key signature without alteration.

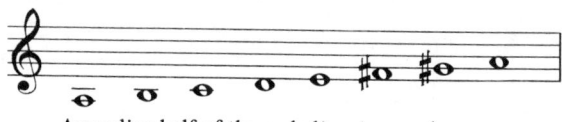

Descending half of the melodic minor scale

The ascending half is different. This half resembles the major scale in all but one tone, the third step. That third step is flatted in order to preserve the minor quality of the melody. Otherwise all minor qualities would be eliminated. (Note that steps 6 and 7 are raised, exactly as in the A-major scale.)

Ascending half of the melodic minor scale

It is not uncommon for minor **melodies** to use this scale, but the harmonies for that melody will use the notes of the harmonic minor. In fact, the harmonic minor is
♦ most often employed for harmonizing rather than creating a melody.

The Skill Builders begin in frame 347. Please turn there now.

There was a mistake in that alternative. Let's look at it. The first thing that needs to be done is to determine the key, then to fix the numbers for each scale degree, and finally, to establish the note names for each tone. These three steps are taken on the staff below.

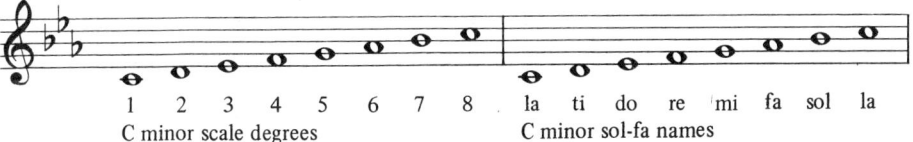

Here is the alternative you chose. When you compare the syllables here with those on the staff above, you will see that the last two syllables are incorrectly identified.

Although it is not necessary to write out the scale degrees and syllables the way they are shown in the top staff on this page, it is necessary to fix them in your mind. Otherwise there is no way to check the alternative's accuracy.

Return to frame 343 and answer the question again.

There was a mistake in that alternative. Let's look at it. The first thing that needs to be done is to determine the key, then to fix the numbers for each scale degree, and finally to establish the note names for each tone. These three steps are taken on the staff below.

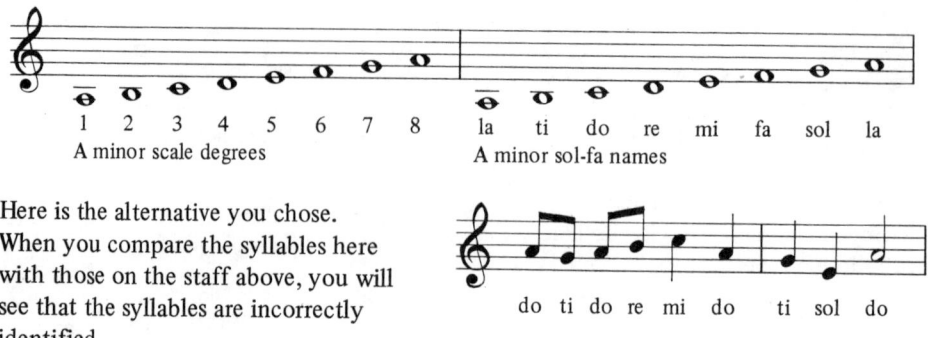

Here is the alternative you chose. When you compare the syllables here with those on the staff above, you will see that the syllables are incorrectly identified.

Although it is not necessary to write out the scale degrees and syllables the way they are shown in the top staff on this page, it is necessary to fix them in your mind. Otherwise there is no way to check the alternative's accuracy.

Return to frame 343 and answer the question again.

347

Skill Builders

1. On the staff lines below, complete the following steps:
   a. Put the treble clef sign of the staff.
   b. Write in the key signature for D minor.
   c. Write the notes of the D natural minor scale.
   d. Write in the notes of the tonic, subdominant, and dominant chords.
   e. Designate them correctly as major or minor triads, using upper- or lowercase roman numerals as needed.

2. What is the relative minor key for each of these major keys?

   F major =   G major =

   B♭ major =   C major =

3. Sing "Shalom, Chaverim" with words, then with sol-fa syllables, using the minor names introduced in frame 341.

SHALOM CHAVERIM

PRONUNCIATION: shalom = shah-loam; chaverim = ha-veh-rim (gutteral H); lehit = lay-hit; raot = rah-oht.

Turn to the next frame.

348

4. Sing "When Johnny Comes Marching Home" with words. Then sing it again with sol-fa syllables, using the minor names introduced in frame 341.

WHEN JOHNNY COMES MARCHING HOME

Continued in frame 349.

Verse 2. The old church bells will peal for joy, Hurrah, Hurrah!
To welcome home our darling boy, Hurrah, Hurrah!
The village lads and lasses gay,
With roses they will strew the way,
And we'll all feel gay when Johnny comes marching home.

Verse 3. Get ready for the jubilee, Hurrah, Hurrah!
We'll give the heroes "three times three," Hurrah, Hurrah!
The laurel wreath is ready now
To place upon his loyal brow,
And we'll all feel gay when Johnny comes marching home!

5. On the preceding page, the chords for "When Johnny Comes Marching Home" are indicated above the staff. Write the notes of each chord on the empty bass clef staff, putting one chord in every measure.

COCKLES AND MUSSELS

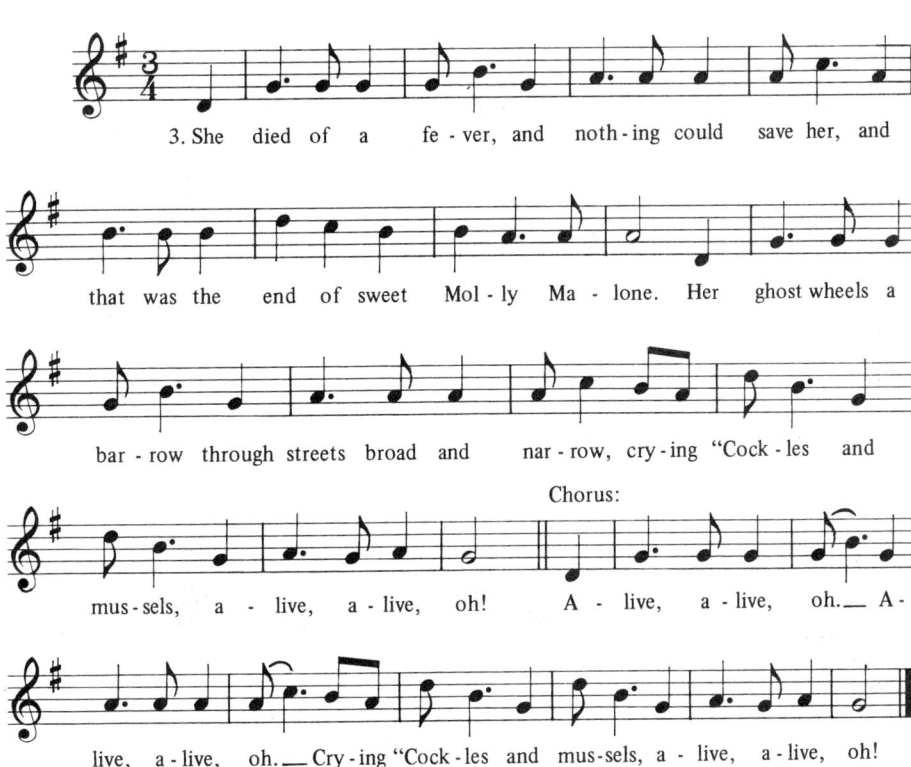

Continued on the next page.

6. The last verse of "Cockles and Mussels" is frequently sung in G minor rather than G major. Convert the third verse below to minor by writing in flats before the appropriate notes. Then sing all of the verses, each in its appropriate tonality. The original song is found in frame 241.

WHAT SHALL I DO WITH A DRUNKEN SAILOR?

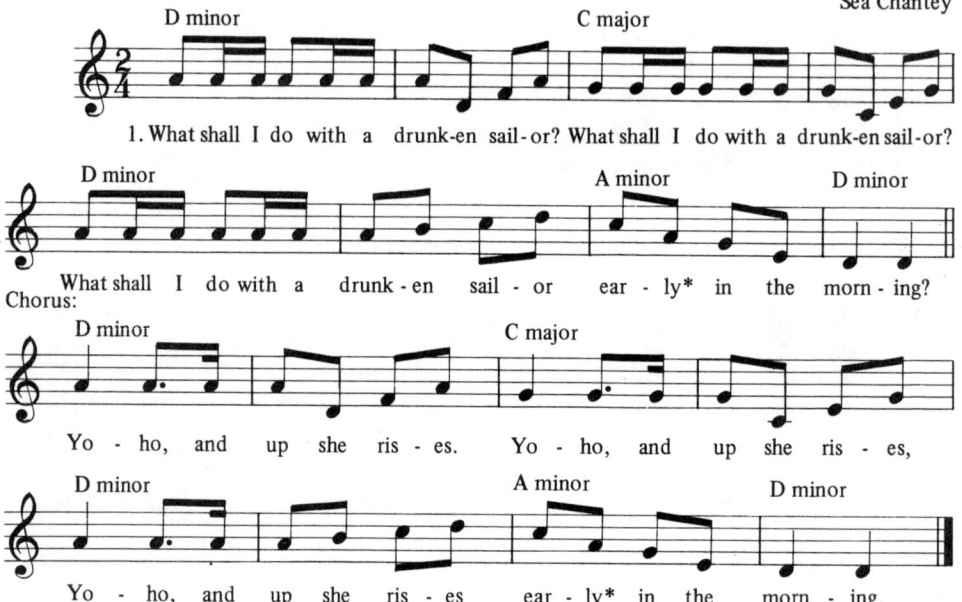

Sea Chantey

*Pronounced EAR-LYE

Verse 2. Put him in a long boat 'til he's sober.
(repeat)

Verse 3. Pull out the plug and wet him all over.
(repeat)

Verse 4. Put him in the bilge and make him drink it.
(repeat)

Verse 5. Tie him to the scuppers with the hose pipe on him.
(repeat)

Verse 6. Shave his belly with a rusty razor.
(repeat)

Verse 7. Keel haul him 'til he's sober.
(repeat)

"What Shall I Do With a Drunken Sailor?" is used in the Self-Test (frame 351). Turn there now.

351

Self-Test

Mark the following statements with T for true or F for false.

1. ____ Steps 3 to 4 and 7 to 8 are half steps in the harmonic minor scale.
2. ____ There are several kinds of minor scales.
3. ____ The I, IV, and V chords of the major key become minor chords in the natural minor key.
4. ____ Steps 2 to 3 and 5 to 6 are half steps in the natural minor scale.
5. ____ The fourth and fifth tones of the major scale remain the same in the minor scale.
6. ____ A minor triad has a minor third for its bottom interval.
7. ____ Every major scale has a relative minor scale.
8. ____ The only difference between the natural minor and the harmonic minor scales is that the third tone of the harmonic minor is one half step lower.
9. ____ In the natural minor scale, steps 3, 6, and 7 have been lowered from the major scale.

Answer the following questions:

10. ____ Is the melody of "When Johnny Comes Marching Home" (part 348) in the natural or harmonic minor?
11. ____ In which minor scale are the primary triads i, iv, and V? (natural or harmonic minor)

Examine the song "What Shall I Do With A Drunken Sailor?" (frame 350) to answer these questions.

12. ____ Is the song in the harmonic minor?
13. ____ Is the song in the natural minor?

Continue the test in the next frame.

14. ____ What is the relative minor of G major?

15. ____ What is the relative major of G minor?

Identify each of the *minor* keys represented by the three key signatures that follow.

16. ____

17. ____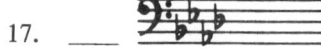

18. ____

19. ____ Relative keys (i.e., relative major or minor keys) are two keys that have the same ____ ____.

20. ____ In the D-harmonic minor scale, the i chord will contain which three notes?

21. ____ In the D-harmonic minor scale, the iv chord will contain which three notes?

22. ____ In the D-harmonic minor scale, which three notes will the V chord contain?

23. ____ An important characteristic of the leading tone is that it is only (*how far*) from the tonic in the harmonic minor?

24. ____ The note G on this staff is on what scale step of the minor key represented by the key signature?

25. ____ What chord is this in the minor key represented by the key signature?

Now that you have completed the test, turn to frame 353 for the Answers and Review Index. After reviewing every question you missed, proceed to Chapter 7. If you missed numerous answers, you should probably reread Chapter 6.

Turn the page for frame 353.

Answers & Review Index

1. F (harmonic minor, 335)
2. T (different kinds of minor scales, 329, 344)
3. T (chords of minor keys, 324)
4. T (half steps in minor keys, 317–318)
5. T (characteristics of minor scales, 317–318)
6. T (minor triads, 217)
7. T (relative major and minor keys, 315)
8. F (characteristics of the harmonic minor, 329)
9. T (characteristics of the natural minor, 317–318)
10. natural (characteristics of the natural minor, 317–318)
11. harmonic (harmonic minor chords, 335)
12. no (characteristics of the harmonic minor, 329)
13. no, it is in the Dorian mode, a scale we have not discussed (characteristics of the natural minor scale, 317–318)
14. E minor (relative major and minor keys, 315)
15. B♭ major (relative major and minor keys, 315)
16. D minor (minor key signatures, 325)
17. F minor (minor key signatures, 325)
18. F♯ minor (minor key signatures, 325)
19. key signature (relative major and minor keys, 318)
20. D-F-A (chords in minor keys, 324, 335)
21. G-B♭-D (chords in minor keys, 335)
22. A-C♯-E (chords in minor keys, 335)
23. one half step (harmonic minor scale, 329)
24. third (minor key signatures, 325)
25. i chord (chords in minor keys, 324, 335)

7
The Structure of Music

===== 354 =====

In the same way that we can examine the tools, equipment, and raw materials used in the construction of a house, we have examined many of the materials used in the construction of music. It is now necessary to examine briefly how these materials can be put together, i.e., how a musical structure is formed.

In this chapter, you will be working to accomplish the following.

Objectives

1. Recognize the definitions of motive, phrase, period, and sequence.
2. Identify motives, phrases, periods, and sequences in musical contexts.
3. Recognize definitions for each of the following terms: AB form, two-part song form, ABA form, three-part song form, binary, ternary, and free form.
4. Identify several of the above forms in musical contexts.
5. Identify three kinds of cadences: half cadence, authentic cadence, plagal cadence.
6. Describe the relationship between cadences and phrases.

Achievement of this chapter's objectives will help you become a more perceptive listener and furnish insight into the constructional procedures used in writing music. Moreover, it should increase your understanding of musical principles and your appreciation of the art form. Although it is beyond the scope of this book to deal at length with form in music, the rudimentary forms presented here will provide the basis for understanding other, more sophisticated forms.

There are six Diagnostic Questions in this chapter.

Turn to frame 355.

355

Diagnostic Question One

On the left are four terms that describe segments of music. See if you can correctly match them with the definitions on the right.

1. phrase
2. sequence
3. period
4. motive

A. a series of notes that leads to, and reaches, a place of resolution or repose

B. a brief musical idea or gesture of a few notes length

C. a combination of two or more phrases

D. a musical fragment repeated several times, each time at a different pitch level

Alternatives

frame

a. I would only be guessing if I matched them. Where is the explanation?   356

b. 1 = B
    2 = D
    3 = A
    4 = C   357

c. 1 = A
    2 = D
    3 = C
    4 = B   359

d. 1 = D
    2 = A
    3 = B
    4 = C   358

The smallest unit in music, called a *motive*, is a short musical idea or a gesture. It is usually only a few notes in length. In "Polly Wolly Doodle," the chorus begins with a motive:

The term *phrase* is the most commonly mentioned unit in music. A phrase is a series of notes that progresses to a point or resolution or repose, frequently at a cadence point. A phrase is sometimes compared to the grammatical unit of a sentence. An example from "Polly Wolly Doodle" with two phrases follows:

Two phrases will frequently fit together as a unit to form a *period*, as illustrated in the example above. A period is the largest of the units considered here. In order of size from the smallest to largest, the units are: motive, phrase, period.

Now turn to frame 363.

357

You must have overlooked something. Please go to frame 356.

358

You have made a mistake somewhere. Please go to frame 356.

359

Absolutely right. Now we want to identify these terms in musical examples. For that, answer the following Diagnostic Question.

Diagnostic Question Two

Which of the following alternatives correctly designates a motive, phrase, and period in the song on the following page?

Alternatives

		frame
a.	From number 4 to number 5 is a motive. From number 3 to number 4 is a phrase. From number 1 to number 4 is a period.	361
b.	From number 5 to number 6 is a motive. From number 6 to number 7 is a phrase. From number 5 to number 7 is a period.	362
c.	From number 7 to number 8 is a motive. From number 6 to number 7 is a phrase. From number 7 to number 9 is a period.	364

(Continued from the previous page.)

POLLY WOLLY DOODLE

Southern Folk Song

Verse 2. Oh my Sal, she is a maiden fair, etc.
   With laughing eyes and curly hair, etc.
   CHORUS

Verse 3. Behind the barn, upon my knees, etc.
   I thought I heard a chicken sneeze, etc.
   CHORUS

Verse 4. He sneezed so hard with whooping cough, etc.
   He sneezed his head and tail right off, etc.
   CHORUS

Verse 5. Oh a grasshopper sitting on a railroad track, etc.
   Just picking his teeth with a carpet tack, etc.
   CHORUS

360

Diagnostic Question Three

A musical concept closely allied to phrases is that of cadences. *A cadence is a series of chords that conveys the feeling of musical conclusion.* Cadences are found at the end of phrases, sections of music, or complete pieces. Three of the more common cadential patterns are identified below. Match each of them with the correct chord progression on the right.

1. plagal or amen cadence   A. progression from V to I

2. authentic cadence   B. progression from I to V

3. half cadence   C. progression from IV to I

Alternatives

		frame
a.	Rather than guess, I would like to read the explanation.	369
b.	1 = A 2 = C 3 = B	366
c.	1 = C 2 = A 3 = B	367
d.	1 = A 2 = B 3 = C	370

You have correctly identified a motive, a phrase, and a period. The next Diagnostic Question is in frame 360.

That was not quite right. Let's look at your choice. In the song in frame 359, from number 5 to number 6 is indeed a motive. From number 6 to number 7 is too brief to be a phrase. (It could almost be called a motive itself.) From number 5 to number 7 could not be a period unless number 5 to number 6 were a phrase and number 6 to number 7 were another phrase. (A period consists of two consecutive phrases.)

Return to frame 359 and answer the question.

A *sequence* is a musical fragment that is repeated several times, each time at a different pitch level. You could make a sequence of five repetitions of the "Polly Wolly Doodle" motive above by treating it this way:

Now return to frame 355.

That was not quite right. Let's look at your choice. From number 7 to number 8 is much too long to be a motive. From number 6 to number 7 is too brief to be a phrase. (It could almost be called a motive itself.) From number 7 to number 9 is more correctly called a phrase.

Return to frame 359 and answer the question.

That was not the correct alternative. The song construction is as follows:

1. From 1 to 2 is an antecedent phrase ending on V.
2. From 2 to 3 is a consequent phrase ending on I.
3. From 3 to 4 is an antecedent phrase ending on V.
4. From 4 to 5 is a consequent phrase ending on I.
5. From 1 to 3 and from 3 to 5 are periods with antecedent and consequent phrases.

Return to frame 368 and answer the question correctly after examining the song to determine where you made the mistake.

You have selected the wrong alternative. Please turn to frame 369 for an explanation.

Excellent. Let's examine some of the chord relationships in these cadences.

The authentic cadence produces the most secure feelings of rest. The reasons for its particular effect lie with the properties of the tones involved. To begin with, the cadence ends on the tonic or I chord. The root of that chord is the tonic note of the key, the note of greatest repose. The strength of the authentic cadence lies equally with the chord that precedes the tonic, namely, the dominant or V chord.

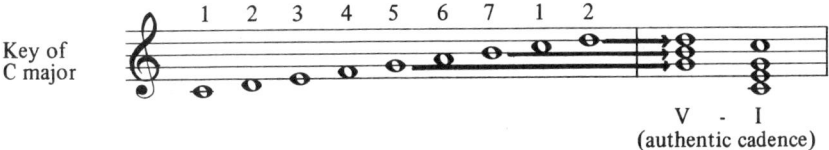

As seen in the illustration above, the V chord consists of tones 5, 7, and 2 of the scale. (See frame 255 for a review of the tendencies of tones.) Of those tones, 2 wants to move down to 1, 7 wants to move up to 8, and 5 wants to move in either direction to 1. All three tones want to resolve to the tonic, a fact that makes the authentic cadence very strong.

When the two chords are placed in reverse order, the cadential expectations are also reversed. The *half cadence* thereby moves from a position of security to one of expectation by progressing from I to V. The feelings evoked can perhaps be compared to a clause in grammatical construction. The clause stands as a unit in some ways, but is clearly dependent on something else for completion. The half cadence is similarly constructed. (Please continue in frame 371.)

368

Diagnostic Question Four

True or False?

In the following song "Swing Low, Sweet Chariot," from one to three is a period with antecedent and consequent phrases, and from three to five has the same periodic construction.

Alternatives

		frame
a.	The statement is true.	382
b.	The statement is false.	365

SWING LOW, SWEET CHARIOT

Spiritual

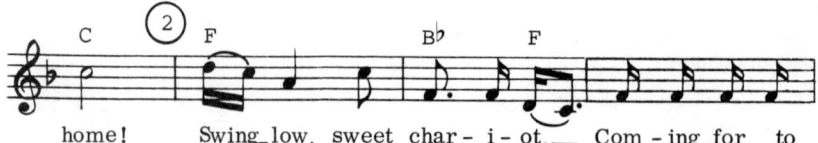

Verses 2, 3, 4 are found on the next page.

Continued from the previous page.

Verse 2. If you get there before I do, coming for to carry me home,
Tell all my friends I'll be there too, coming for to carry me home.

Verse 3. The brightest day that ever I saw, coming for to carry me home,
When Jesus washed my sins away, coming for to carry me home.

Verse 4. I'm sometimes up and sometimes down, coming for to carry me home.
But still my soul feels heavenly bound, coming for to carry me home.

CADENCES: A variety of cadences have been devised over the years in order to develop varying degrees of finality at cadence points. Some cadences evoke very strong feelings of conclusion. Others evoke feelings of a brief pause, but not of final conclusion.

The most secure cadence is the progression from the V chord (or V_7) to the I chord. It is called the *authentic cadence*. A less pronounced feeling of conclusion is created with progression from IV to I. This cadence is the *plagal* cadence or the *amen* cadence, so named because so many hymns use it on the word "amen" at the hymn's conclusion.

The most common cadence for brief or momentary rest is the half cadence. It is obtained by reversing the order of the authentic cadence (V–I) so that the phrase ends on the dominant chord (I–V). By ending on the V chord, feelings of further musical activity are evoked in the listener.

To review the three cadences:

1. authentic cadence = V to I
2. plagal (amen) cadence = IV to I
3. half cadence = I to V

Return to frame 360 and answer the question.

That was not the correct alternative. Please turn to frame 369 for an explanation.

CADENCE CHECK: Three cadences are identified below in songs found earlier in the book. Look up each cadence and determine its nature. Write the correct term in the column on the right, selecting from authentic, plagal, and half cadences as possibilities.

                                                         Type of Cadence
                                                         (write your answer here)

1. "Michael Finnigin" (frame 304), measures 2–4.   _____

2. "Michael Finnigin" (frame 304), measures 7–8.   _____

3. "A Frog Went A Courting," (frame 302), measures 6–8.   _____

4. "A Frog Went A Courting," (frame 302), measures 14–16.   _____

(Check your answers now with the key found at the bottom of frame 384.)

Let's examine another concept related to phrases and cadences. In "Oh Susanna," (frame 372), the song starts on the tonic chord of the key (F), and progresses to the dominant seventh (C_7) of the word "knee." That cadence ($I-V_7$) is a half-cadence, and marks the first place in the song where a feeling of repose is established. In this case, the repose is momentary because of the nature of the cadence. The second phrase of "Oh Susanna" employs an authentic cadence, which establishes a more complete sense of repose at number 3. The two phrases together form a period.

A period consists of two phrases. The first one most frequently ends with some kind of a half cadence and a feeling of expectancy. That phrase is known as an *antecedent phrase*. The second phrase in the period ends with a secure feeling of finality and is known as a *consequent phrase*. The antecedent-consequent phrase construction in periods is widely found, and is frequently referred to as a question-and-answer construction.

Turn to the Diagnostic Question in frame 368.

372

OH SUSANNA

Stephen Foster

Continued from the previous page.

Verse 2. I had a dream the other night, when everything was still,
I thought I saw Susanna a-coming down the hill.
A buckwheat cake was in her mouth, a tear was in her eye,
says I, "I'm coming from the south, Susanna don't you cry."
CHORUS

=== 373 ===

Diagnostic Question Five

Phrases of a song can be organized in many different ways to create different kinds of forms.

Listed on the left are six musical forms with a blank after each of them. On the right are three descriptions, lettered A through C. Write the proper letter after each of the terms on the left. (Some of the letters will be used more than once.)

1. binary   ____
2. ABA   ____
3. free   ____
4. ternary   ____
5. AB   ____

A. A form frequently referred to as two-part song form. It consists of two main sections of music both of which may be repeated.

B. A song form that follows no set pattern and is not repeated.

C. This is a three-part song form. It involves the idea of establishing a melody, going to something new, and returning to the first melody at the conclusion.

After writing in your answers, turn to frame 377 and grade them. Then continue the program in that frame.

=== 374 ===

You have chosen the wrong alternative. Please read the analysis of the song in frame 375.

375

If you examine lines 1, 2, and 4 of the song (frame 379), you will see that these musical lines are almost exactly the same. These phrases must, therefore, be labeled with the letter A.

A	A		A
line 1	line 2	line 3	line 4

Only line 3 is different. It would, therefore, be identified as B. The form, then, is AABA, which is usually simplified to ABA, or ternary form.

Now return to frame 379 and see if you can detect this form in the song.

376

You are right. The song has ternary form (AABA). Listed below are several songs that employ the forms we have discussed. It would be beneficial for you to examine them to determine where the phrases are and why they are classified under that particular form.

Binary Form

"This Old Man," frame 52
"Go Tell Aunt Rhody," frame 53
"On Top of Old Smoky," frame 377
"Polly Wolly Doodle" (verse), frame 359

"Billy Boy," frame 191
"Clementine"*
"Yankee Doodle" (verse), frame 115
"Auld Lang Syne"*

Ternary Form

"The More We Get Together," frame 379
"Twinkle, Twinkle Little Star"*
"Au Clair de la Lune," frame 378

"Old MacDonald," frame 55
"Alouette," frame 190
"All Through the Night"*

Free Form

"America the Beautiful," frame 239
"A Frog Went A-Courting," frame 302

"When Johnny Comes Marching Home," frame 348

Turn to frame 381.

*These songs are not in this book, but are common examples of the form indicated.

Your answers in frame 373 should read as follows:

1. (binary) A
2. (ABA) C
3. (free) B
4. (ternary) C
5. (AB) A

Binary form consists of two different phrases, the prefix bi- in binary indicating two parts. If the first phrase is identified as A, the second phrase would be identified as B. Therefore, the form is also known as AB form. The form is identified with a third name, *two-part form.* An example of this form is found in the following song:

ON TOP OF OLD SMOKY

Verse 2. For courting's a pleasure, and parting is grief,
But a false hearted lover is worse than a thief.

Verse 3. A thief will just rob you, and take what you have,
But a false hearted lover will lead you to the grave.

Verse 4. They'll hug you and kiss you, and tell you more lies,
Than ties on a railroad, or stars in the skies.

In "On Top of Old Smoky" phrase ① begins the song and ends on the word "snow." Phrase ② starts with the word "I" and goes to the end. Any song that consists of two different phrases may be called two-part, or binary form.

Turn to the next frame.

Three part or *ternary* song form is one of the most important forms in music and perhaps the most frequently used. The word *ternary* means divided into three parts, and can be described with three words: establish, depart, and return. Using this form, a composer establishes a melody in part A, then leaves that melody to introduce a new one in part B. When this second part is completed, the music returns to the original melody, repeating the first phrase. The following diagram illustrates the ternary principle:

A	→	B	→	C
first part		second part		first part repeats

The first phrase of ternary song form is frequently repeated so the form is actually AABA. A good example is found in the following French folk song.

AU CLAIR DE LA LUNE

In "Au Clair de la Lune," the first line is phrase A, and the second line is a repetition of the first. The third line begins a new melodic idea, and is phrase B. The fourth line is once again a repetition of the first line, giving the song an AABA format, still termed a ternary form. Go to the next frame.

Thus far we have discussed two forms: (1) binary and (2) ternary. Another form, *free form* (occasionally referred to as "through composed") has no predictable order. It may consist of any number of phrases, each one different from the former ones. If letters were assigned to each new phrase, the form would be ABCDE and so forth.

Diagnostic Question Six

Examine the song shown below and determine its form. Then select your alternative.

THE MORE WE GET TOGETHER

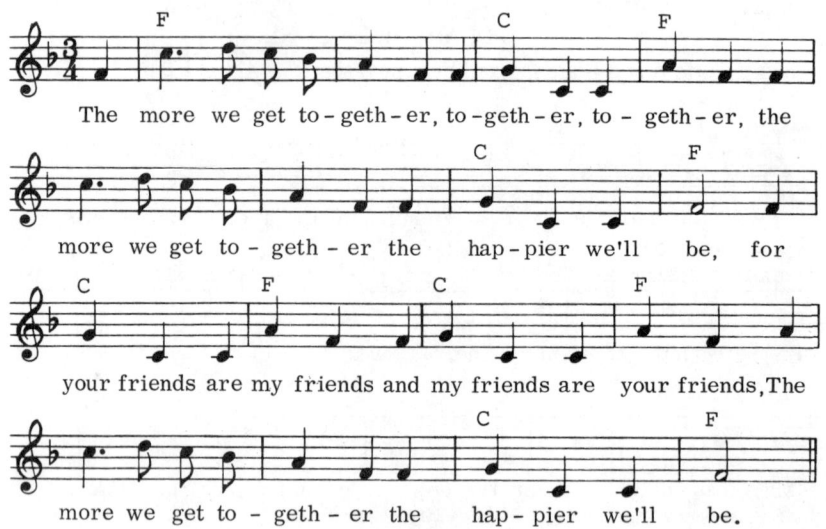

Alternatives

		frame
a.	Please explain the answer.	375
b.	This song has binary form.	374
c.	This song has ternary form.	376
d.	This song has free form.	380

380

You chose the wrong alternative. Please read the information in frame 375.

381

The forms just discussed were all illustrated with relatively short folk tunes, but they have much wider application. Indeed, longer musical compositions performed by classical soloists, chamber ensembles, or full orchestras employ these same forms regularly. For example, binary form is utilized in much of the music written between 1600 and 1750 (e.g., the music of Bach and Handel). Frame 382 is a well-known excerpt from Johann Sebastian Bach, *Orchestral Suite no. 3 in D Major*. The excerpt is titled "Air" and is in binary form. Parts A and B are marked by repeat signs: ‖:A:‖ ‖:B:‖.

Go to frame 383.

382

You are right. The song construction is as follows:

1. From 1 to 2 is an antecedent phrase ending on V.
2. From 2 to 3 is a consequent phrase ending on I.
3. From 3 to 4 is an antecedent phrase ending on V.
4. From 4 to 5 is a consequent phrase ending on I.
5. From 1 to 3 and from 3 to 5 are periods with antecedent and consequent phrases.

Turn to frame 373 and continue the program.

AIR from ORCHESTRAL SUITE NO. 3 in D MAJOR*

Johann Sebastian Bach
(1685-1752)

Continued on the following page.

Continued from the previous page.

Turn to frame 384.

*From Edition Eulenburg no. 818. Reprinted by permission of C. F. Peters Corp., sole selling agents in the U.S.A.

Ternary form is even more widely used. An expanded version of the form is the basis of many movements of symphonies, particularly first movements. In this expanded format, a large section of music is presented, new musical material is introduced, and then the original music is brought back again in slightly altered form. Instead of ternary, it is called *sonata-allegro* because of its predominant use in the allegro movements of sonatas and the fact that many other musical devices are employed.

Here is the melody line from part of Haydn's "Symphony No. 94 in G Major," the third movement. The movement is not in sonata-allegro form, but this section is ternary. The initial presentation and the return to the "A" section (slightly altered) have been marked.

Turn to frame 385.

CADENCE CHECK ANSWERS
(*from frame 371*)

Type of Cadence

1. half cadence
2. authentic cadence
3. half cadence
4. plagal cadence

SYMPHONY NO. 94 in G MAJOR, THIRD MOVEMENT

Franz Josef Haydn
(1732-1809)

Turn to frame 386.

You have now completed Chapter 7. Before proceeding to the self-test, do each of the activities described below. They will help you retain the knowledge just acquired and translate it into useable skills.

Skill Builders

1. Turn to "America the Beautiful" (frame 239) and identify the four phrases of the song. song. Then identify their cadences with roman numerals and by name.

2. Try identifying phrases and cadences in the song "When Johnny Comes Marching Home" (frame 348), which is in a minor tonality.

3. With your left hand play the I chord in a key of your choice on the piano, followed by the V chord. Then do it again while creating your own melody with the right hand. The melody will probably sound best if you begin and end on some note of the chord being played. Try it several times. Then reverse the cadence (V to I) and do the same thing.

4. Identify the forms of at least five songs in another song book.

5. Turn to each song listed in frame 376 and identify the properties that give it its form.

6. Turn to the song "The Naughty Boy" in frames 387–388. Examine it carefully and determine the form.

7. How many phrases are there in "Tallis' Canon" below? Why do you say there are that number, and not more or fewer?

TALLIS' CANON

THE NAUGHTY BOY*

John Keats
Edmund F. Soule

*Used with permission, Edmund F. Soule, University of Oregon, Eugene, Oregon.

(Continued in the next frame.)

The Self-Test begins in frame 389.

389

Self - Test

On the left are eight musical terms, and on the right are six definitions. Pick the correct definition for each of the terms. (Some definitions will be used more than once.)

1. _____ motive
2. _____ ternary form
3. _____ free form
4. _____ period
5. _____ AB form
6. _____ phrase
7. _____ ABA form
8. _____ binary

A. a form frequently referred to as two-part form, consisting of two main sections of music, both of which may be repeated

B. a brief musical idea or gesture of a few notes length

C. a series of notes that leads to, and reaches a place of resolution or repose such as a cadence

D. a form that follows no set pattern and does not repeat phrases

E. a combination of two phrases

F. a three-part song form involving the idea of establishing a melody, going to a new melody, and then returning to the original

9. What principle is the basis of the ternary form?

Turn to frame 390 and answer the questions based on the following song.

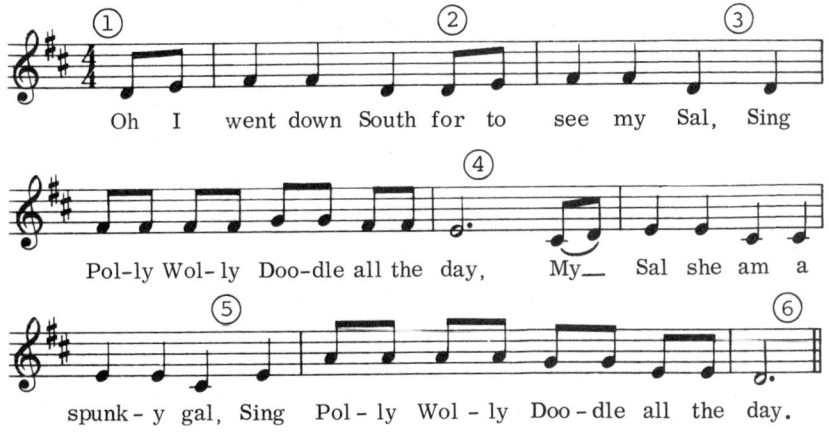

Turn to frame 390.

10. ____ What term is used to describe the unit of music between numbers 2 and 3?

11. ____ What term is used to describe the unit of music between numbers 1 and 4?

12. ____ What is the form of this section of song? (binary, ternary, or free)

13. ____ What term is used to describe the unit of music between numbers 1 and 2?

14. ____ What term is used to describe the unit of music between numbers 4 and 6?

15. ____Which is longer—a phrase or a period?

16. What is the word we give to the harmonic progressions that help determine phrase endings?

17. Turn to the excerpt from Haydn's "Symphony No. 94" (frame 385). Early in the chapter we defined sequences. Locate sequences in *two* places in the excerpt.

18. In the following musical excerpt identify the end of the antecedent phrase and the beginning of the following consequent phrase.

SYMPHONY NO. NINE, FOURTH MOVEMENT

Ludwig van Beethoven
(1770–1827)

19. In the following musical excerpt, identify the end of the antecedent phrase and the beginning of the consequent phrase.

SYMPHONY NO. 1, LAST MOVEMENT

20. On the following page is the song "Old Dan Tucker." What is the form of the song?

Turn now to the Answers and Review Index in frame 393. Review every question you missed by looking up the appropriate part of the program and reading the question. Then check the question to see if you can select the appropriate response. If you missed numerous questions you should reread Chapter 7.

OLD DAN TUCKER

American folk song

1. I came to town the oth-er night, I heard the noise and saw the fight. The

watch-man he was a-run-ning round say-ing "Old Dan Tuck-er's come to town._

Chorus:

Get out the way, Old Dan Tuck-er, get out the way,_ old Dan Tuck-er,

Get out the way, old Dan Tuck-er, you're too late to come for sup-per.

Verse 2. Now old Dan Tucker was a fine old man
He washed his face in a frying pan.
He combed his hair with a wagon wheel
And died with a toothache in his heel.
CHORUS

Verse 3. Now old Dan Tucker and I fell out,
And what do you think it was all about?
He borrowed my old setting hen,
And wouldn't bring her back again!
CHORUS

Verse 4. When old Dan Tucker came to town
He'd swing the ladies all around.
He'd swing them right and swing them left,
Then swing the one that he liked best.
CHORUS

Answers & Review Index

1. B (motive defined, 356)
2. F (ternary form, 378)
3. D (free form, 379)
4. E (period, 356, 371)
5. A (AB form, 377)
6. C (phrase, 356)
7. F (ABA form, 378)
8. A (binary form, 377)
9. The principle of ternary form is "something is stated, there is a departure from it, and then it returns." (ternary form, 378)
10. motive (identified, 356, 359)
11. phrase (identified, 356, 359)
12. binary form (identified, 377, 381, 383)
13. motive (identified, 356)
14. phrase (identified, 356)
15. period (length of, 356, 371)
16. cadences (described, 360, 369)
17. Sequences are found in the following places:
    —a series of 3; beginning with line 2, measures 4–5
    —a series of 3; beginning with line 5, measure 1, last note
    —a series of 7; beginning with line 5, measure 5
    (sequences identified, 356)
18. antecedent phrase ends at end of 4th measure (antecedent–consequent phrases, 371)
19. antecedent phrase ends after the 3rd beat of measure four (antecedent–consequent phrases, 371)
20. AABB or binary (binary form, 377)

Appendix

394

MAJOR KEYS: SIGNATURES, SCALES, AND CHORDS

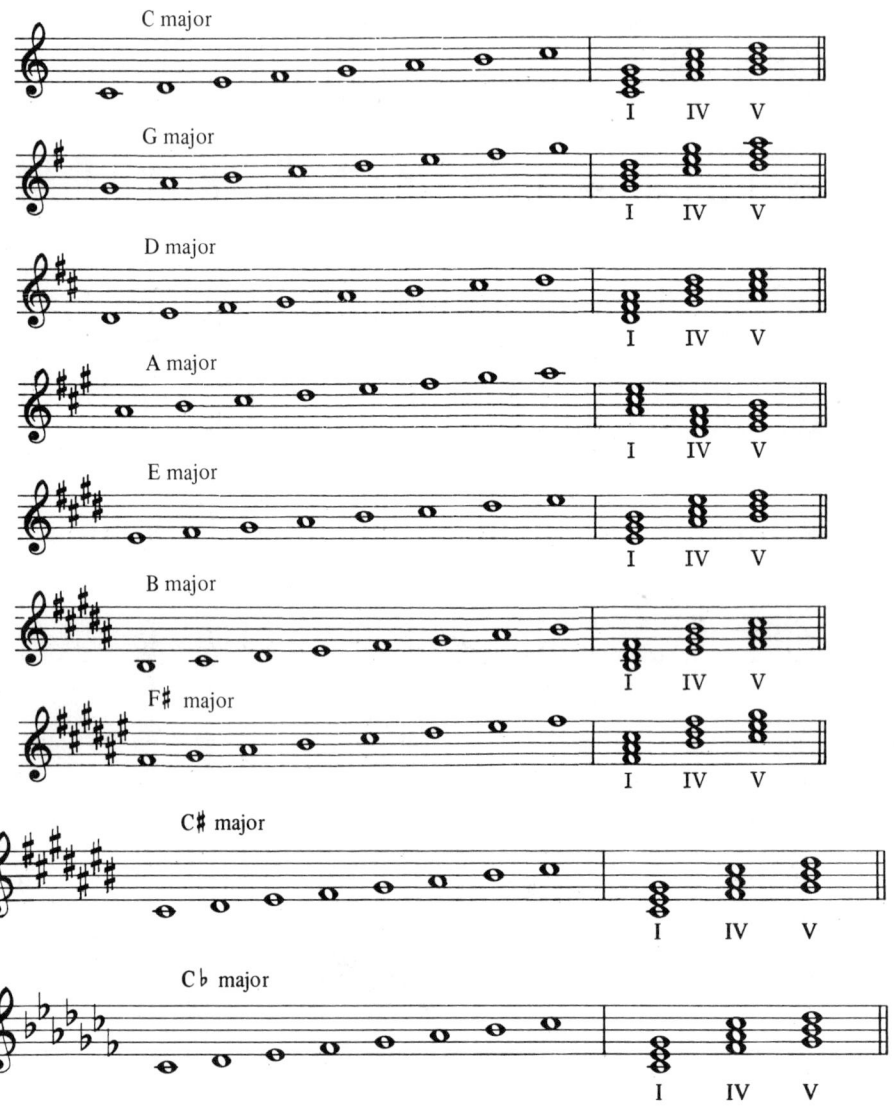

HARMONIC MINOR KEYS: SIGNATURES, SCALES, AND CHORDS

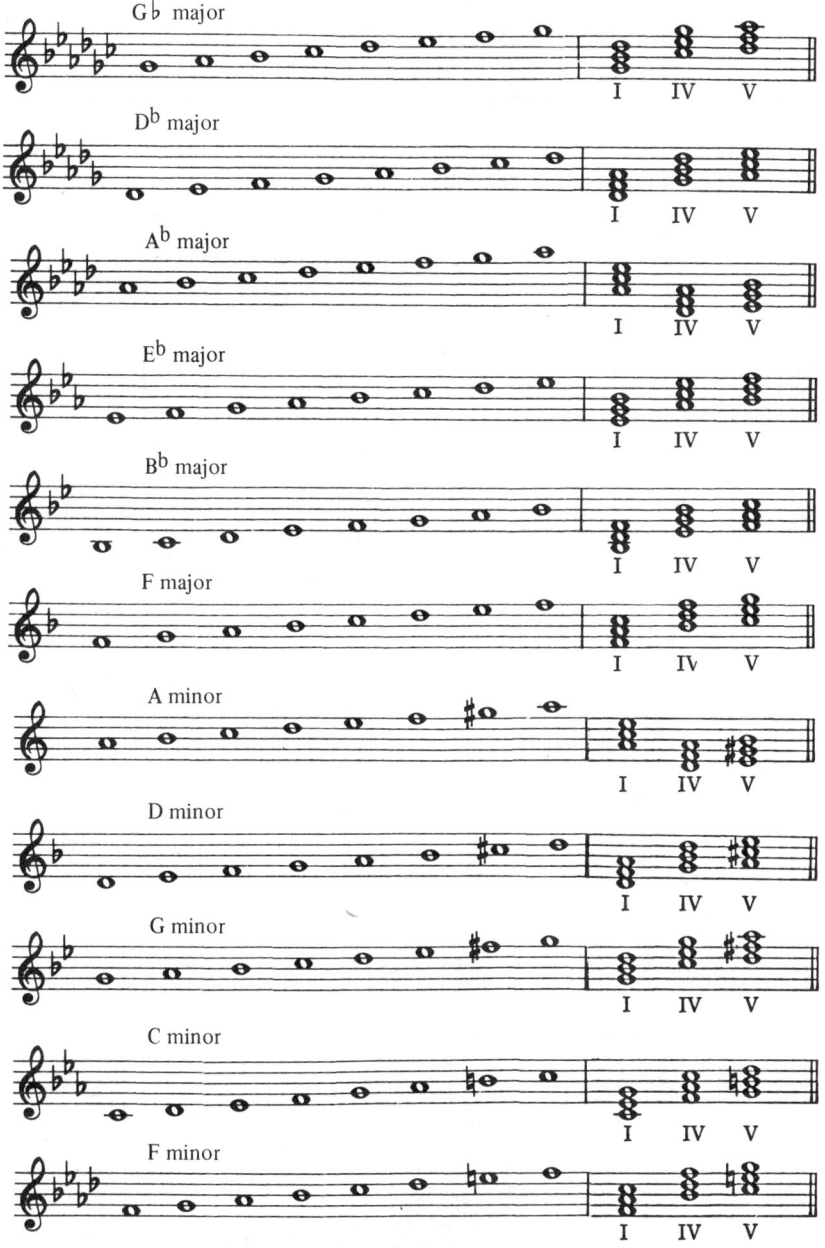

396

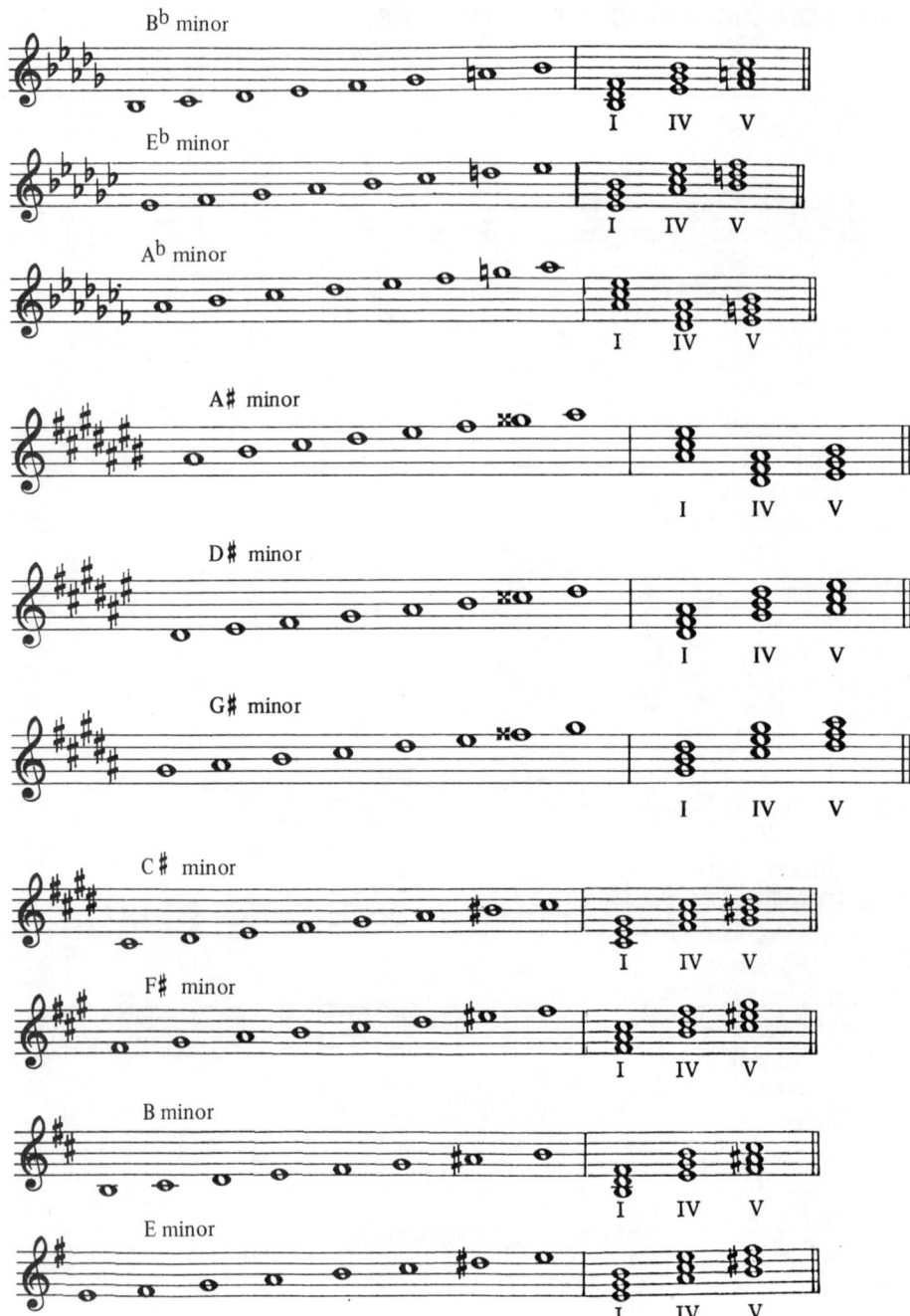

Song Index

	frame
A Frog Went A-Courting	302
Alouette	190
America the Beautiful	239
Au Claire de la Lune	378
Billy Boy	191
Bingo	53
Cockles and Mussels	241, 349
Farmer in the Dell	117
Go Tell Aunt Rhody	53
Heigh-ho Nobody's Home	342
Lili Ou Kalani	305
Little Tom Tinker	118
Magic of Christmas, The	242
Michael Finnigin	304
Muffin Man, The	303
Naughty Boy, The	387
O Come, O Come Emmanuel	112
Oh Susanna	372
Old Dan Tucker	392
Old MacDonald Had a Farm	55
On Top of Old Smoky	377
Orchestral Suite No. 3, "Air" (J. S. Bach)	382
Polly Wolly Doodle	359
Reuben and Rachel	243
Shalom Chaverim	347
Swing Low, Sweet Chariot	368
Symphony No. 94, Third Movement (Franz J. Haydn)	385
Tallis' Canon	386
The More We Get Together	379
There Was a Woman Old and Gray	189
This Old Man	52
What Shall I Do With a Drunken Sailor?	350
When Johnny Comes Marching Home	348
Yankee Doodle	115

Index of Terms

AB form, 377, 381
ABA form, 378
accent mark, 105
antecedent phrase, 368, 371

bar lines, 7
bass clef
    notes, 138
    sign, 6
binary form, 377, 381

cadence
    authentic, 369, 367ff
    defined, 360
    half, 369, 67ff
    plagal, 369
calligraphy, musical, 45
chords
    defined, 199
    dominant seventh, 300
    inversions, 231
    minor, 324, 335
    names, 295, 300
    primary in key, 295
    substitutes, 298
circle of fifths
    major, 274
    minor, 325
compound meters, 113
consequent phrases, 371, 368
crescendo, 40

da capo, 36
dal segno, 36

decrescendo, 40
dominant chord, 295, 300
dominant seventh chord, 300
dotted notes, 73
double whole note, 51
dynamic markings, 39

eighth note, 14
eighth rest, 28

fine, 36
flats, 162
form
    binary, 377, 381
    free, 379
    ternary, 378

grand staff, 6

half note, 14
half rest, 28
half steps, 158
harmonic intervals, 203
harmonic minor chord, 335
harmonic minor scale, 329
harmony, defined, 199

interval
    defined, 203
    harmonic, 203
    inversions, 202, 212
    sizes, 201

key
  definition, 249
  relative, 315, 318
  signatures, 268, 325
  tone, 249
keyboard
  black key names, 167
  white key names, 144

ledger lines, 133

major scale construction, 260
major third, 218
measure, 7
melodic intervals, 203
meter, 65
meter signatures, 87
meter, compound, 115
meter, simple, 115
minor scale construction, 317, 329
minor thirds, 218
motive, 356

natural, 162
natural minor scale, 317, 335
note values, 14

octave, 175, 176

period, 356, 371
phrase
  antecedent, 371, 368
  consequent, 371, 368
  defined, 356, 359
piano keyboard, 144, 167
pickup notes, 109
pitch, musical, 22, 124
primary chords, 298
pulse, 65

quarter note, 14
quarter rest, 28

relative keys, 315, 318
repeat sign, 30

rhythm, 65
rhythmic note values, 14

scales
  harmonic minor, 332
  major, 249
  natural minor, 317
  relative, 315, 319
scale tones
  names, 287
  numbers, 252
  tendencies, 255
sequences, 356
sharp, 162
simple meters, 113
sixteenth note, 14
sixteenth rest, 28
slur, 80
Sol-fa system
  major, 281
  minor, 341
staccato, 105
staff, 6
subdominant chord, 295

tempo, 65
tenuto mark, 105
ternary form, 378
thirds, quality of, 218
tied notes, 80
time values, 66
tonality, 249
tonic chord, 295
tonic sol-fa system, 281
treble clef
  notes, 126
  sign, 6
triads
  inversions, 231
  quality, 217

whole note, 14
whole rest, 28
  whole steps, 158, 164